Cries in the Night

Women Who Challenged
the Holocaust

Cries in the Night

Women Who Challenged the Holocaust

Michael Phayer
Eva Fleischner

Foreword by Nechama Tec

Sheed & Ward
Kansas City

Sheed & Ward™ is a service of The National Catholic Reporter Publishing Company.

Library of Congress Cataloguing-in-Publication Data
Phayer, Michael, 1935-
    Cries in the night : women who challenged the Holocaust / Michael Phayer, Eva Fleischner : foreword by Nechama Tec.
       p.   cm.
    Includes bibliographical references.
    ISBN: 1-55612-977-7
    1. Righteous Gentiles in the Holocaust—Biography. 2. World War, 1939-1945—Jews—Rescue. 3. Catholic women—Europe—Biography. 4. World War, 1939-1945—Women—Biography. I. Fleischner, Eva, 1925- . II. Title.
D804.65.P48   1997
940.53'18'0922—dc21
[B]   97-24419
                                        CIP

Published by: Sheed & Ward
                  115 E. Armour Blvd.
                  P.O. Box 419492
                  Kansas City, MO 64141-6492

To order, call: (800) 333-7373

www.natcath.com/sheedward

Cover design by Jane Pitz.

Contents

*To Our Students, Who by Learning
About the Holocaust Taught Us a Deeper
Understanding of It*

Foreword

Nechama Tec[1]

WITH THIS SCHOLARLY AND HUMANE BOOK FLEISCHNER and Phayer have given us valuable insights about the meanings and implication of altruistic rescue in general and rescue by Catholic women in particular.

During the German occupation of Europe the presence of Christians who risked their lives to save Jews signaled an opposition to and an interference with the Nazi measures of Jewish annihilation. Because these measures were introduced to different European countries at different times, the appearance of these Christian rescuers also varied with time and locality. Similarly, the efforts required for saving Jews also differed with time and place.

Until recently, the literature about the destruction of European Jews paid little attention to Christian rescue of Jews. This prolonged silence is not surprising. The Holocaust was dominated by extreme suffering and devastation. In these destructive environments the compassion and help

---

1. Nechama Tec has written six widely acclaimed books about the Holocaust. *Defiance: The Bielski Partisans* won the 1994 International Ann Frank Special Recognition prize. *In the Lion's Den: the Life of Oswald Rufeisen* won the Christopher Award in 1991. Two other books, *Dry Tears: the Story of a Lost Childhood*, and *When Light Pierced the Darkness: Christian Rescue of Jews in Nazi-Occupied Poland*, both won the Merit of Distinction Award from the Defamation League of B'nai B'rith. A professor of sociology at the University of Connecticut at Stamford, Tec's next book will deal with women during the Holocaust.

that were a part of the Jewish experience were rare and
easily overshadowed by the enormity of the Nazi crimes.
It is understandable that students of that period would
focus first on the typical, common events rather than the
few exceptional expressions of human goodness. Only
when the basic outlines of the annihilation process were
examined could scholars even begin to notice the less visible, the less obvious; namely, the selflessness and compassion that were expressed in the readiness of some few to
die for others. Once noticed, however, the contrast between
the cruelty of that period and the ability to rise above it to
save the helpless and the hunted only underlines the nobility of these deeds.

My own research on Christian rescuers concentrates
on Poland, a country designated by the Nazis as the center
of Jewish annihilation. Most European Jews were sent to
die there. Poland was also a place to which the Nazis
introduced their measures of destruction early and ruth-
lessly, without regard to human cost. As the center of
Jewish annihilation Poland provides the key to an understanding of the destruction of European Jews in general
and to the rescuing of Jews in particular.

It seems that in Poland and elsewhere most Christians
who risked their lives to save Jews did so without antici-
pation of external rewards. Their actions fit into behavior
identified as altruism. Who were these selfless rescuers?

When I compare a large number of Christian protectors in terms of social class, education, political involvement, degree of antisemitism, extent of religious
commitment, and friendship with Jews, results are very
variable. Some belong to higher, some to lower classes.
Some are highly educated, while others are illiterate. A
similar diversity shows up in their religious and political
commitment and most other conventional categories in
terms of which we tend to classify people. Although a few

of these comparisons seem to offer a partial explanation, none qualifies as a reliable predictor for the protection of Jews.

In contrast to these heterogeneous results, a close view of these selfless rescuers' life styles and behaviors yields a cluster of shared characteristics and conditions which in turn suggests a set of interrelated hypotheses and explanations. I refer to one of these shared characteristics as individuality or separateness. It shows that these rescuers did not quite fit into their social environments; a condition some of them were or were not aware of. Conscious or not, these rescuers' individuality or separateness appeared under different guises and was related to other shared conditions and motivations.

Being on the periphery of a community, whether one is aware of it or not, means being less affected by this community's expectations and controls. Therefore, with individuality come fewer social constraints and a higher level of independence. This, in turn, has other important implications. Freedom from social constraints and a high level of independence offer an opportunity to act in accordance with personal values and moral precepts, even when these are in opposition to societal demands. Thus, to the extent that people are less controlled by their environment and are more independent, they are more likely to be guided by their own moral imperatives, regardless of whether or not these imperatives conform to societal expectations.

Rescuers in my study had no trouble talking about their self-reliance, their need to follow personal inclinations and values. Nearly all of them saw themselves as independent (98%).

With this came the realization that they were propelled by moral values, values which did not depend on the support and approval of others but on their own self-approval.

Again and again they repeated that they had to be at peace with themselves and with their own ideas of what was right or wrong.

An important part of the rescuers' ideas of what was right and wrong, their moral convictions and values, was a long-standing commitment to help the needy. This commitment was expressed in a wide range of charitable acts that extended over a long period of time. Evidence for such selfless acts also came from survivors, most of whom described their protectors as good natured and as people whose efforts on behalf of the needy were limitless and long lasting.

There seems to be a continuity between the rescuers' history of charitable actions and their wartime protection of Jews. That is, risking lives for Jews fits into a system of values and behaviors that had to do with helping the weak and the dependent.

This analogy, however, has its limitations. Most disinterested actions on behalf of others may involve inconvenience, even extreme inconvenience. Only rarely would such acts suggest that the giver has to make the ultimate sacrifice of his or her own life. For these Christian rescuers, then, only during the war was there a convergence between historical events demanding ultimate selflessness and their already established predispositions to help.

We tend to take our repetitive actions for granted. What we take for granted we accept. What we accept, we rarely analyze or wonder about. In fact, the more firmly established patterns of behavior are, the less likely are they to be examined and thought about. Therefore, in a real sense, the constant pressure of, or familiarity with ideas and actions does not mean that we know or understand them. On the contrary, since customary patterns are accepted and taken for granted, this often impedes rather than promotes understanding.

Related to this tendency is another. Namely, what we are accustomed to repeat we don't see as extraordinary, no matter how exceptional it may seem to others. And so, the rescuers' past history of helping the needy might have been in part responsible for their modest appraisal of their life threatening actions. This modest appraisal was expressed in a variety of ways. Many Polish rescuers (66%) saw in their protection of Jews a natural reaction to human suffering, while almost a third (31%), insisted that saving lives was nothing exceptional. In contrast, only three percent described the saving of Jews as extraordinary.

Given these matter-of-fact perceptions of rescue, it is not surprising that aid to Jews often began in a spontaneous, unpremeditated way. Offered gradually or suddenly, these helping activities were neither planned nor anticipated. Indeed, 76% of the Jewish survivors I studied said that the aid they had received happened without prior planning. This unpremeditated start of the helping activity underscores the rescuers' need to stand up for the poor and helpless.

So strong was this need to help, so much was it a part of the rescuers' makeup, that it overshadowed all other considerations. When these protectors were asked why they had saved Jews, they overwhelmingly emphasized that they had responded to the persecution and the suffering of victims and not to their Jewishness. What compelled them to act was the persecution, the unjust treatment, and not the people themselves.

This ability to disregard all attributes of the needy, except their helplessness and dependence, I refer to as universalistic perceptions. Evidence for the presence of these perceptions comes from a variety of sources. One of them is the fact that 95% of these rescuers felt they were prompted to help by the need of the Jews. This is in sharp contrast to the 26% who claim to have helped because it

was a Christian duty, or the 52% who saw their response
as a protest against the German occupation. Clearly, more
than one kind of motivation was involved.

As a group, Christian rescuers who tried to save Jews
selflessly without expectations of concrete rewards were
engaged in altruistic actions.

As we continue to study this historical period, we
ought not lose sight of its rare yet encouraging feature: the
presence of those few who were ready to die for the persecuted and hunted Jews. As someone who has researched
Jewish rescue, as someone who survived the war by passing
for a Catholic, I am convinced that we ought to continue
examining the less visible and less common part of the
Holocaust, the actions of Christians who selflessly rescued
Jews.

Paying attention to these protectors cannot detract
from the study of the millions of Jewish victims. On the
contrary, the lives of Christian rescuers were intricately
connected to Jewish victims. By acknowledging the presence of these courageous protectors we fill significant gaps
in the knowledge of that period. By finding out more about
Christians who risked their lives to save Jews we gain a
more complete picture of the Holocaust.

To focus only on the devastation and inhumanity of
the Holocaust to the exclusion of the noble and the good,
may in the long run have the effect of a self-fulfilling
prophecy. I agree with Jan Karski, a righteous Christian,
who in one of our private conversations argued persua-
sively about the significance of public awareness about
Christians who risked their lives to save Jews.

Karski thinks that, in addition to teaching us history,
the very presence of these rescuers tells that, although the
Jews were abandoned by all governments, they were not
abandoned by all the people. It also clearly shows that some
Christians felt that Jews were worth dying for. In itself this

kind of a message combats not only the negative images of Jews but also antisemitism.

The presence of Christian rescuers points to other important conclusions. These Christians made a difference. They saved lives. This in turn shows that participation in selfless rescue of Jews, while dangerous, was possible. In a way, by taking part in the dangerous protection of Jews these rescuers point to missed opportunities. The situation was not totally helpless. Others could have helped as well. More could have been done. In short, instead of excusing the bystanders, awareness of the selfless protection of Jews only underlines the bystanders' failure to help. Had some of those who claim that nothing could have been done engaged in rescue, fewer Jews would have perished.

Additional but different arguments can also be made in favor of the study of altruistic rescue of Jews. Persecutions, discrimination, and prejudice are a part of our everyday life. More often than not those who are victims of these negative forces cannot effectively fight back. Knowing who would stand up for the persecuted and the helpless, knowing what factors are involved in the protection of the poor, the dependent and the downtrodden, creates an opportunity for cultivating such positive forces.

Finally: we live in a shaky and uncertain world, a world that offers little help in choosing life values. In such a setting, knowledge and awareness of noble and self-sacrificing behaviors may help restore some shattered illusions. Indeed, mere awareness that in the midst of ultimate human degradation some people were willing to risk their lives for others denies the inevitable supremacy of evil. With this denial comes hope.

With their book, a most welcome and important contribution to the field, Fleischner and Phayer have taken a giant step toward the fulfillment of these expectations.

Introduction

THIS BOOK IS ABOUT LIGHT, "LIGHT THAT PIERCED THE DARK-ness,"[1] the darkness that was the Holocaust. The purpose of this introduction is to give this light its proper context. For it is not light but the very opposite, an almost impenetrable darkness, that characterizes the Holocaust, or *Shoah*.[2] We must first turn to this darkness before we speak of the light that pierced it now and then.

In his book, *The Abandonment of the Jews*, historian David Wyman points out that it was not the lack of workable plans that stood in the way of saving thousands, perhaps millions, of European Jews. Nor was it the lack of ships, or the fear that rescue efforts would hamper the war effort. "The real obstacle was the absence of a strong desire to save Jews."[3] In other words, the world did not care.

Of course there was Hitler, there were his henchmen. There were those who conceived and operated the death camps, who gave the orders, who kept the trains running. There were the murderers. But millions could have been saved if the world had not stood by; if the leaders of the

---

1. *When Light Pierced the Darkness* is the title of Nechama Tec's study of Christian Rescuers of Jews in Nazi-occupied Poland.
2. The word "Holocaust" is being applied so widely and generally to catastrophes of all kinds that it is in danger of losing its meaning. We prefer to use the term *Shoah* (Hebrew for "whirlwind") for the murder of Europe's Jews under Hitler. The word will not be italicized hereafter.
3. David S. Wyman, *The Abandonment of the Jews. America and the Holocaust 1941-1945.* New York: Pantheon Books, 1984, p. 339.

Allies and of the Churches had spoken out. If the Shoah is indeed, in the words of Franklin Littell, the watershed of this century, then apathy is perhaps the greatest sin of our age.

As one listens to the chronicle of opportunities lost, of all that might have been done and was not done, one comes close to despairing of human nature. And yet, there is light in the almost impenetrable darkness that was the Shoah, a light that emanates from those who refused to stand by, who risked their lives to save Jews. They are the women and men whom Jewish tradition honors with the title, "Righteous among the Nations." The great avenue leading up to Yad Vashem is named in their honor the Avenue of the Just,[4] and each tree lining it bears the name of a rescuer.

It was Jews who pioneered the effort to keep alive the memory of these men and women. One of the earliest, and perhaps the most visible, of these efforts is to be found at Yad Vashem, where since 1953 the Department of the Righteous, with a full-time staff paid by the Israeli government, spares no effort to collect any documentation that can be found on those who saved Jews, so that their memories may be honored. We refer not only to Yad Vashem, however. We recall books such as Philip Friedman's *Their Brothers' Keepers*; Philip Hallie's *Lest Innocent Blood be Shed*, the story of the French mountain village, Le Chambon-sur-Lignon, that became a "city of refuge" for thousands of Jews, a story that is movingly portrayed in a film by Pierre Sauvage; Nechama Tec's *When Light Pierced the Darkness*, a study of Polish rescuers; the study of Samuel and Pearl Oliner, *The Altruistic Personality*; Mordecai Paldiel's *The Path of the Righteous*; Fay Block and Malka Drucker's *Res-*

---

4. Yad Vashem: Documentation Center and memorial to the victims of the Shoah, located on Mount Herzl outside Jerusalem.

cuers; Eva Fogelman's *Conscience and Courage.*[5] The authors
of all these books, and of many others that could be mentioned, are Jews; as is the founder of the Foundation for
Righteous Gentiles, Rabbi Harold Schulweis.[6]

In recent years these Jewish voices have been joined
by the voices of non-Jews, Christians among them.[7] Christian scholars are latecomers to this field, which is as it
should be. Indeed, some of them have questioned whether
they have any right at all to speak about rescuers, especially
Christian rescuers. For Christians have much to atone for
vis à vis Jews and Judaism, also – and especially – during
the time of the Shoah. We refer here to the ancient history
of Christian anti-Judaism, to what has come to be known
in our time as the Teaching of Contempt. Although the
term is relatively recent – it was coined by the French
historian Jules Isaac who lost part of his family in Ausch-

---

5. Philip Friedman, *Their Brothers' Keepers.* New York: Holocaust Library,
   1973; first published in 1957. Philip Hallie, *Lest Innocent Blood be Shed.*
   New York: Harper & Row, 1979. Samuel P. And Peal M. Oliner, *The
   Altrustic Personality.* Rescuers of Jews in Nazi Europe. New York: The
   Free Press, 1988. Mordecai Paldiel, *The Path of the Righteous.* Gentile
   Rescuers of Jews during the Holocaust. Hoboken, N.J.: KTAV Publishing
   House, 1993. Nechama Tec, *When Light Pierced the Darkness.* New York:
   Oxford, 1986. Fay Block and Malka Drucker, *Rescuers. Portraits of Moral
   Courage in the Holocaust.* New York: Holmes & Meier, 1992. Eva Fogelman,
   Conscience and Courage. New York: Anchor, 1994.
6. Rabbi Harold Schulweis is the founder of the Jewish Foundation for
   Christian Rescuers/ADL. The Foundation exists for the purpose of providing help to rescuers who, in their old age, have inadequate financial
   resources. More than any other single individual Rabbi Schulweis is
   responsible for work being done in the U.S. on rescuers.
7. To mention only a few: Carol Rittner and S. Myers, eds., *The Courage to
   Care.* New York: New York University Press, 1986. D. Huneke, *The Moses
   of Rovno.* New York: Dodd, Mead, 1985. A. Ramati, *The Assisi Underground:* The Priests who Rescued Jews. New York: Stein & Day, 1978.
   Fernande Leboucher, *Incredible Mission: The Story of Fr. Marie Benoit, Who
   Rescued Thousands of Jews from the Gestapo,* 1970. Hiltgunt Zassenhaus,
   Walls. Boston: Beacon Press, 1974. Varian Fry, *Assignment: Rescue: An
   Autobiography.* Scholastic Press and the U.S. Holocaust Memorial Mu-
   seum. David P. Gushee, *The Righteous Gentiles of the Holocaust: A Christian
   Interpretation.* Minneapolis: Fortress, 1994.

witz (cf. pp. 99ff below) – the phenomenon it describes is almost as old as Christianity. Let us briefly summarize it.

The Teaching of Contempt, found in liturgy, preaching, catechesis and theology, has for nearly two thousand years presented the Jewish people as spiritually dead: cursed, punished and cast aside by God because they had rejected the Messiah. By the early second century the decided charge had been formulated, whereby Jews – all Jews, down through the centuries – were accused of being Christ-killers. Jews thus came increasingly to be seen as enemies of God, as allies and agents of the devil. As the Church became identified with the temporal power of the Roman empire these attitudes were concretized in anti-Jewish legislation, and frequently led to discrimination and accusations of blasphemy and ritual murder; these in turn prompted persecution, expulsion, and mass slaughter. Few if any of Hitler's anti-Jewish measures were invented by him. They lay ready at hand in the arsenal of the medieval church, and could simply be brought out of storage.

While the Teaching of Contempt is not sufficient in and of itself to account for the Shoah, a number of theologians and historians, Christian as well as Jewish, have cogently argued that it helped prepare the soil for Hitler's all-out "war against the Jews." The schema proposed by Raul Hilberg is well known: to the medieval Church's attempt to solve the "Jewish question" through conversion or, that failing, through expulsion from their native countries, the Nazis added a third step, annihilation.[8]

We quote here two other authors in support of this thesis. Rosemary Ruether writes:

> The Nazis . . . were not Christian. They were, indeed, anti-Christian. . . . Nevertheless, the church must bear

---

8. Raul Hilberg, *The Destruction of the European Jews*. Chicago: Quadrangle Books, 1961, pp. 3 and 4.

a substantial responsibility for a tragic history of the Jew in Christendom which was the foundation upon which political antisemitism and the Nazi use of it was erected. (*Faith and Fraticide*, p. 184)

In the words of Canadian scholar William Nicholls:

Nazi antisemitism was anti-Christian as well, and it passed beyond all Christian or even human limits, but it would never have arisen without the Christian past, of which it was the secular offspring. Without the inheritance of "knowledge" that Jews were bad, there could have been no Holocaust.
(*Christian Antisemitism: A History of Hate*, p. 3)

Christians must face this heavy burden of their own history. Only if they try to do so can there be hope of a new beginning and the possibility of forging a new relationship with the people that constitutes the very root of Christianity.[9]

In this effort to confront the shadow-side of their tradition Christians can be helped by the knowledge that there were individuals – lay women and men, priests and religious, bishops – who recognized in the persecuted Jews their brothers and sisters, and who risked their lives to help them. Yad Vashem has honored some 12,000 persons to date. We shall never now how many others there were

---

9. Fortunately, in our time a new beginning has been made. Starting with the Second Vatican Council and its epoch-making declaration, *Nostra Aetate* in 1965, the Roman Catholic Church affirmed its Jewish roots, and rejected the decide charge and the accusation of collective guilt of Jews for the death of Jesus. This has been followed by numerous church documents, both from the Vatican and from individual episcopal bodies, urging Catholics to renounce antisemitism and to discover for themselves the richness of Judaism. These developments in the Roman church are paralleled by those in many other churches. Rabbi James Rudin of the American Jewish Committee has called Jewish-Christian dialogue "the success story of the twentieth century." One can only hope that history will prove him right.

besides these "officially" recognized ones; many are dead, we do not even know their names. Even if there had been hundreds of thousands, their number is still small when compared with the ocean of apathy, with the millions who cooperated with the killers. Let us remember, however, that goodness is not measured in numbers. As Jewish tradition taught long ago, "Whoever saves one life, it is as though he/she had saved the whole world." The same lesson is taught by the ancient legend of the thirty-six Just.

This book is being written at a time when the subject of rescuers has been given new prominence through the extraordinary success of the film "Schindler's List." While we are aware of the potential danger of focusing on this one man who saved Jews, and making him a symbol of the attitude of Germans in general (cf. *The Sunday New York Times*, June 12, 1994, pp. 1 and 6), we believe that the story of rescuers must continue to be told. One risks being overwhelmed by the darkness of the Holocaust. We need to know that there was some light after all.

The stories of the women told in this book begin in Poland, where the Holocaust took place. Thus Matylda Getter's rescue efforts take us into the very heart of what the Holocaust was all about. From Poland we move to Germany and to Margarete Sommer's valiant, and often frustrating, struggle to arouse the German hierarchy. Margit Schlachta tried to stem the tide of destruction of Hungarian Jews. There follow chapters on three French women: Germaine Ribière played an important role in Christian resistance to Nazism, and heroically tried to save Jews with or without the backing of the French hierarchy. Marie Rose Gineste, a social worker, was involved in personal rescue of Jews, as well as a trusted collaborator of Bishop Thèas of Montauban, one of the first French bishops to protest publicly the persecution of Jews. Germaine Bocquet gave refuge to Jules Isaac, who while in hiding wrote his ground-breaking book, *Jesus and Israel*, and coined the term "the Teaching of Contempt" for Christian antisemitism through the centuries. Years later Isaac played a crucial role in persuading Pope John XXIII to put the church's relation to Judaism on the agenda of Vatican II. We return to Germany with Gertrud Luckner, whose tireless efforts directly contributed to Vatican II and *Nostra Aetate*, and who shared the fate of Nazi victims in Ravensbrück.

In choosing these seven women from among many others we might have chosen we admit to a personal bias. All of them are Roman Catholic lay women who, without the benefit of theological training, knew what is right and did it. Nor did it end there. Sommer pushed the German bishops to persuade the pope to act. Schlachta personally went to Rome and begged Pius XII to intervene on behalf of Hungarian Jews. . . . In this day and age, when women continue to find themselves shut out of decision-making roles in their church, their stories deserve to be told.[10]

They raise some questions for us: What motivated the heroic rescue work of these Catholic women? What tensions between their faith and the institutional church did they live with? What made them willing to remain within the church they loved, yet which so often failed them? What lessons regarding the role of women in the church can we draw from the experience of these women? Some tentative answers to these questions may emerge at the end of this book.

A word of caution to those among our readers who, like the authors, teach the Holocaust to college students.

---

10. It should be pointed out that Protestant no less than Catholic women opposed Hitler and on many occasions tried to save Jews. Magda Trocmé, honored by Yad Vashem, is one of many who comes to mind. Cf. also "Women and the Protestant Church Struggle," in Michael Phayer, *Protestant and Catholic Women in Nazi Germany*, Detroit: Wayne State University Press, 1990, pp. 129 ff.

We have struggled for years with the question, at what moment in our teaching should we speak of the rescuers? If the subject is raised early in the course it can become a means of escape, of avoiding the apathy and evil that are the dominant notes of the Holocaust. Years of teaching the subject have convinced us that this chapter of Holocaust history may be dealt with only relatively late in the semester's course, after students and teacher have struggled to confront the failure of their religious and national communities to come to the aid of European Jews. Only if given its proper place in our teaching can the subject of rescue provide us with models of goodness, and affirm our hope in humanity's future.

A note to our readers.

You will find a marked difference in style between the chapters written by Michael Phayer and Jessica Scheetz (chapters 1, 2, 3, and 8) and those by Eva Fleischner (chapters 4, 5, and 6). Phayer's work reflects extensive archival research and study of documents. The chapters by Fleischner, on the other hand, have the immediacy of personal encounters, and of friendships that developed subsequently. Rather than try to blend our styles we made the decision to give each other the freedom to write in the way he or she felt best-suited to their material. This was the only way in which we could truly be co-authors. We hope our different styles will complement each other, and that our readers will appreciate, rather than be frustrated by, the variety of tone and style of this book.

Chapter One

The Innocent Eyes of Children

Looking back, it seems simple. To save Jews during the Holocaust a Christian needed only to remember that they were children of God, created in His image. But most people evaded this basic truth. A Polish nun, Matylda Getter, acting unhesitatingly on this simple tenet of faith, saved hundreds of Jews.

Getter was already 70 years old when the Second World War began in the fall of 1939. The war trapped Jews in Europe, three million of whom lived in Getter's Poland. Having already been much honored by both the church and the government of Poland for her social work, the elderly Getter need not have defended Jews against Hitler's murderers. Not to do so never entered her mind.

Rescuing Jews was dangerous work. Those whom the Nazis caught harboring Jews paid immediately with their lives. To encourage the sisters of her order to continue to risk their lives to save Jewish children, Mother Matylda Getter told them to look into the beautiful, innocent eyes of Jewish children.[1]

---

1. For much of the material in this chapter I am indebted to Sister Teresa Fracek, RM, who provided me with bibliographical references on Getter, and with her own essays which are based on archival material of the house archives of the Sisters of Mary in Warsaw. Much of the material in this chapter was derived from Fracek's paper on Getter of March 2, 1992, delivered in Warsaw for the Edith Stein Society.
   I am also indebted to Derek Ciemniewski, a doctoral candidate at Marquette University, who generously spent many hours translating Polish historical material for me.

Most of the atrocities that befell European Jews took place in Poland. After the Hitler-Stalin pact in 1939 Polish Jews were forced into ghettos, where they lived literally on top of each other. Many died of malnutrition and disease. When Hitler betrayed Stalin and attacked Russia in 1941, Mobile Killing Squads (the *Einsatzgruppen)* were assigned to accompany the army for the purpose of murdering Jews right where they lived. Finally, when they decided to eliminate all European Jews, the Nazis built six great killing centers in 1942, all of which were located in Poland. Thus, the great majority of Europe's Jews were murdered and their bodies cremated in Nazi-occupied Poland.

Clearly, Jews in Poland lived in terror. To Mother Matylda Getter it was obvious that hundreds of thousands of the Nazi victims would be tiny infants and little children. Her concern was natural since her religious order, the Sisters of the Family of Mary, had operated homes for orphaned children all over Poland long before the Nazi occupation.

In saving Jews Getter let her beliefs and convictions guide her. Jews were human beings; it did not matter if they were not Christian. On the supernatural level, Getter told her sisters that by saving Jews they were saving their own souls.

On the practical side, Getter's working principle was her conviction that any child who came to one of her convents had been sent there by God. These simple, uncomplicated guidelines allowed Getter and her sisters to act boldly and resourcefully in defiance of the Nazis.

Orphaned Jewish Children

How exactly did the children come to Mother Getter and her convents? Most commonly, they were brought to her or to one of the convents by the child's Jewish parents.

After ghettos were formed in larger cities – the Lodz and Warsaw ghettos were established already in April and November, 1940, respectively – this would no longer have been possible. But babies and little children could still be smuggled out of the ghetto. The mother house of the Sisters of the Family of Mary, located across the street from one of the Warsaw ghetto's entrances, was ideally situated.[2] The parish priest of All Saints church, located just inside of the larger Warsaw ghetto, smuggled Jewish infants out. Other children, not yet ghettoized, were brought to the orphanages by Polish civil employees.

Once children found relative safety within convent walls, Getter and her sisters had to provide new identities for them. The chief of social services in Warsaw, Jan Starczewski, assisted them. Getter would get phony baptismal certificates from sources like Father Marceli Godlewski of All Saints parish, and then process them through Starczewski's social service office.[3] Although the Nazis suspected what was going on (Starczewski was later arrested), Getter's method gave her Jewish children the protection they needed.

After the Warsaw ghetto was sealed off from the rest of the city toward the end of the year 1940, more and more Jewish refugee families were packed into it. These newcomers were especially at risk of death by starvation and cold. Emmanuel Ringelblum, the chronicler of the Warsaw ghetto, recorded how hungry, preschool-aged street children whimpered by day on the ghetto sidewalks and died there at night.

---

2. Stanislaw Swiderski: "Dzialalnosc charytatywna Kosciola Wsród Zydów W Warszawie W Latach Okupacji," *Materialy I Studia*, ed. Franciszka Stopniaka. Warsaw: Akademia Teologii Katolickiej, 1978, 3, 252-263.

3. Regarding Godlewski, see Nechama Tec, *When Light Pierced the Darkness*. New York: Oxford University Press, 1986, ch. 4.

A Polish social welfare worker, Jan Dobraczynski, tried to direct as many children to the famous orphanage of Janusz Korczak as possible. A crisis arose in January of 1941 when the Germans wanted to clear the Warsaw ghetto of begging street children. Their numbers were so great that these children could not be accommodated in Korczak's home. Consequently, roughly 2500 children from the Warsaw ghetto were placed by Dobraczynski in cooperating convents of Warsaw.[4] Many of these children were taken to the Family of Mary convent just outside the Warsaw ghetto. From there they were dispersed to other homes of the Family in Warsaw and outlying Polish provinces.

It sometimes also happened that older children found their way to Mother Getter on their own. One Holocaust survivor, Lilia, recalled first meeting Mother Getter as a young girl in the convent garden and saying to her, "I don't have any place to stay; I am a Jew without rights." Getter responded, "My child, whomever comes into our yard and asks for help, we cannot refuse in the name of Christ."[5] For Lilia this memory was more vivid than any other of the war; years later she wrote, "I will never forget this moment."

Many of the orphanages of the Family of Mary had been situated in smaller cities or rural settings of Poland. These made ideal refuges in which to hide Jewish children.[6] In addition to their remoteness, it was advantageous to have so many homes because it meant that Jewish children could be interspersed with a much larger number of Catho-

---

4. Franciszka Stopniaka, *Materialy I Studia*. Warsaw: Akademia Teologii Katolickiej, 1981, 5, 45ff.

5. Letter of Lilia Engle to the Sisters of the Family of Mary, December 20, 1983.

6. Orphanages where Jewish children were placed were located in Pludy, Anin, Vialoleka, Brwinow, Kostowiec, Miedzylesie, Zosinek, Ulanowek, Pustelnik, Izabelin, Wola, Golkowska, Kostowiec, Brwinow.

lic children. This made it much more difficult for the Nazis to ferret out the Jews, and, had they ever succeeded in doing this, only a relatively few of the sisters' children would have been lost. Having many homes located long distances from each other also made it possible for Getter's sisters to transfer orphans, whom the Nazis suspected of being Jewish, from one part of Poland to another.

In the summer and fall of 1942 the Nazis transported most of the Jews of the Warsaw ghetto to the gas chambers of Treblinka. The Warsaw ghetto rebellion ensued. During these events an estimated 8,000 Jews escaped the ghetto and found refuge on the outside.[7] The fate of Jewish orphans worried Adam Czerniakow, head of the Jewish council in Warsaw. It is likely that he undertook to get as many of these children out of the ghetto as he could, before he himself was overcome by the desperateness of the entire situation and committed suicide in July.

The number of Jewish orphans in Getter's care surged during this ghastly time. In one orphanage alone, Pludy, the number of Jewish girls rose from 40 to 100.

Good Faces, Bad Faces

Rescued children were sent one by one from Warsaw to an orphanage in a more remote area of Poland. Ethnic features partly determined to which home a child would be sent. Children spoke of having a "good face" or a "bad face" depending upon how Jewish they looked. Those with "bad faces" were in a state of panic, but all of the children were fearful of what was happening around them.

Frightened by the Nazi terror, by the prospect of being separated from home and family, and by the idea of living among total strangers, Jewish children suffered from acute anxiety. The sisters of the Family worked to quiet their

---

7. Leni Yahil, *The Holocaust*. New York: Oxford University Press, 1990, 380.

fears, but they were themselves fearful of Nazi reprisals. Although fear was an ally against relaxing – against giving away one's ethnic secret – it was accompanied by stress, anxiety, and shame.

Nazi terror generated the fear. What started out as cruel taunting of Hassidic Jews – cutting off beards and locks – escalated into arbitrary brutality. On the sidewalks of Warsaw for all to see, Jews were kicked, beaten and even shot. What began as over-crowding in the ghetto (about half a million people jammed into an area just slightly more than one square mile) escalated into unsanitary living conditions, starvation and typhus. Jews died in such numbers that corpses, both of children and adults, lay for days on the streets and sidewalks of ghettos. Beyond the basic fear of deprivation of home and loved ones, everyday street scenes terrified little children.

Young women of an employable age and adults could cope with less anxiety. Supplied by Getter with false identities, these women could live like other Poles, and sometimes even find employment in a Family of Mary orphanage. One survivor recalled that Getter sent her to work in a provincial orphanage where the Catholic personnel "suspected who I was but they never let me feel different, treated me very well and were very friendly."

Another survivor, Mary Eckerling, came in desperation to Getter's convent just outside the Warsaw ghetto and told her "the police are after me and I cannot go back to my apartment. I am a Jew and don't know what to do with my life; my heart cries out despondently."[8] Getter put the young woman up that same night in the convent. Later, after testifying that Eckerling had been raised by the sisters of the Family, Getter found work for her in another convent.

---

8. Mary Eckerling to S. Fracek, Paris, Nov. 9, 1983. Eckerling kept the name, "Mary," that the sisters gave her; Eckerling is her married name.

Younger children, who could not begin to grasp the enigma of Nazi genocide, needed to be warned to be on their guard. But since they were already frightened by being separated from their parents and placed in strange surroundings, the sisters first had to calm the children, win their trust, and reassure them.

There were three especially dangerous situations: when the Nazis held impromptu inspections of an orphanage; when a child was transferred from one home to another; and when an orphan needed to be taken to a hospital or doctor. The children shivered and trembled when Germans were around. Eventually, a bond between the sisters and children formed, and the nuns could concentrate on preparing them so that they would be taken for Christian.

Not only the children were afraid. The sisters who sheltered them feared for their lives. Mother Getter, who encouraged her sisters to hide Jewish children but did not require them to do so, was herself at times deeply troubled or afraid. Getter's secretary noticed that she shook like a leaf at times. Some Poles – including, possibly, some of the sisters – objected to what Getter was doing, saying she had no right to endanger the religious personnel and the non-Jewish Polish orphans. What right, Getter must have asked herself, did she have to urge her sisters to heroic acts when the church itself was silent?

An incident arose during the Nazi terror in Poland that brought Getter's internal conflict to a crisis. She grew fearful when a young woman from the orphanage in Pludy inadvertently revealed her Jewish heritage, and it became known outside of the orphanage. Someone then began to menace the sisters with blackmail. "This caused deadly threats to everyone at the Pludy home."[9] Even before this

---

9. Maria Miklewicz, formerly a Jewish orphan, to Mother Helena Kaniak, Aug. 12, 1968.

incident the Nazis, who had become suspicious of the orphanage, threatened the nuns and beat some of them. One
sister was even put before a firing squad that feigned her
execution.

The leak from the Pludy orphanage upset Getter ter-
ribly. She wondered if she should remove all of the Jews
from the Pludy home in order to save others. But this would
have jeopardized the lives of the Jewish children. After
agonizing over the situation for some while, Getter told a
confidant, Maria Miklewicz, that

> I prayed for a long time and asked Jesus what His will
> was in this matter and I understood that I should not
> remove anyone from the Pludy orphanage including
> the woman who made the slip. I still have to protect
> the Jewish children from Nazi hands; let our safety be
> in God's hands. I know now what my obligation is and
> I have regained peace of mind.[10]

Getter's decision proved fortunate; the Nazis did not learn
about the presence of the Jewish woman.

Jewish Children and Christian Culture

If they were not to fall into Nazi hands and die, Jewish
children had to learn the Christian prayers that other Polish
youth knew by heart. They also had to attend all of the
religious services that took place in the orphanage, because
their ethnicity was kept secret from the other children. Even
though Jewish children realized that learning Christian
prayers and actions (like genuflecting or making the sign
of the cross) could save their lives, their involvement with
Christianity often did not remain artificial.

Not infrequently, it led to religious questioning, if not
downright doubt, about their Jewish faith. After Jewish

---

10. House archives; letter of Maria Miklewicz to Mother Helena Kaniak,
n.p., Aug. 12, 1968.

children overcame their fear and developed a close, personal bond with the sisters, what these adult, parental figures thought and did was bound to influence them. As orphanage personnel it was the duty of the sisters to attend to the education and character formation of those in their care. It could not be helped that the sisters' immature Jewish wards fell under the religious influence of the nuns even if they did not intend it.

In addition, the very fact that survival depended on the religious convictions of the sisters was bound to have an impact on Jewish children. Mary Eckerling put it this way:

> I had a "bad face" and was therefore frightened as I stood before the convent house in Zelazna street. I felt that the drama of my life would be resolved by Getter – I felt this. And when I stood before Getter I felt that the heavens had opened before me.

All children are impressionable and the circumstances surrounding the Jewish children during the Holocaust increased the likelihood of their being influenced by the authority figures of the Polish Christian world in which they found themselves.

The thoughts and feelings of Janina Dawidowicz illustrate how a young Jewish girl would react to the situation within the orphanage home as the Nazi terror raged outside its walls. "After escaping from the Nazi hell, having lost my trust in people, I entered a world in which I was surrounded by love and I was taught about love and God's love for people. I believed like a Christian because without this faith I could not have survived the coming years."[11]

Janina received her parents' permission to be baptized, a step she felt compelled to make. "My greatest desire in

---

11. House archives of the Sisters of the Family of Mary. Janina Dawidowicz (married name) to Sister Sofia Olszewska, London, Nov. 16, 1974.

Warsaw was to become one with you. This was necessary
to save my life and to save my mind. I needed this kind of
belonging – of being a member of the group – and would
have suffered if I had not been accepted." For Janina baptism became a religious experience with a double significance. "After I was baptized I felt totally free; no one would
harm me and if they did I would go immediately to
heaven."[12]

Obviously, the sisters could have taken advantage of
the situation of the Jewish children. There was, at that time,
a conviction among Catholics that Jews as a people were
damned and that their salvation as individuals lay in conversion. Probably for this reason the sisters did baptize
Jewish babies, but only if they were without either parents
or guardians. If an infant's parents were alive, the sisters
did not baptize it but furnished it with a fake baptismal
certificate.

With children and young girls there was a similar
policy. They were baptized only occasionally and then only
with their parents' permission. For some as yet unknown
reason more girls living in the Pludy home wanted to be
baptized than in others. When a baptism took place under
these circumstances, it was done in secrecy, so that the
other children, whether Jewish or Catholic, were unaware
of it.

Mother Getter did not proselytize Jewish children. In
this respect, she set a policy, or at least an example, for
others to follow. A recollection of Mary Eckerling illustrates
this. "One day," Mary recalled, Mother "Getter gave me a
medallion (blessed medal) saying, 'I know that you don't
believe in this, but I do, so please keep it with you.' "[13]

---

12. Ibid.
13. House Archives of the Sisters of the Family of Mary; Mary Eckerling
    (married name) to Sister Fracek, Paris, Jan. 15, 1984.

Eckerling never converted but she saves the medal to this day. She recalls that Getter had respect for the beliefs of the Jews, and that neither she nor others tried to convince them to convert.

Getter's postwar attitude toward her Jewish children is consistent with her religious treatment of them during the Holocaust. Some of the children did not want to leave the orphanage after the war. Their parents had perished and they preferred the sisters' homes to that of a perhaps distant and unknown relative. Getter believed however that they belonged with their families.

One young girl, Helenka, did not want to join her grandfather in Jerusalem. He had lost all of his family but succeeded in finding his granddaughter, Helenka, through the Red Cross. Getter told Helenka in no uncertain words that "your place is not with me but with your lonely grandfather; if you don't understand this there is no God in your heart." As to faith, Getter said, "there is no Catholic God or Jewish God; there is only one God." Helenka joined her grandfather in Jerusalem.

Halina Harla's experience was similar. After the war she did not want to return to her father because she could not remember him. For her the sisters meant safety. Three times, she later recalled, they had saved her life, twice when the Nazis were inspecting the orphanage and once during the Warsaw uprising when she had an infection and the sisters carried her to a medical station run by Polish insurgents.[14] Halina felt that her place was with the sisters, but they convinced her to join her father in Israel.

After the Jewish children had left the sisters' homes they gradually fell out of contact with the nuns. There were a few exceptions to this, and in all but one of these cases

---

14. House Archives; Lea Balint's (married name) recollection of September, 1984. Balint's alias while in hiding with the sisters was Halina Harla.

the sisters learned that their former wards had returned to their Jewish faith. This did not bother them. Rather, they were pleased to learn that the children's brush with Christianity had left them with positive feelings. As Janina Dawidowicz put it,

> I had believed like a Christian because without this faith I could not have survived the Holocaust years. Despite my future doubts and breakdowns, something has survived in me from those years of faith – if nothing else, I still today have access to this other world which under other circumstances would have been completely closed to me. Although I am no longer practicing, some of my closest friends are Catholics from Ireland and I share a lot in common with them.[15]

Israel Remembers Getter and Her Sisters

During the Holocaust Getter and her sisters rescued at least 500 Jewish children. The number is probably greater but verification exists for roughly this many. In addition, Getter and the Family of Mary sisters concealed 250 or more adult Jews. They were able to do this by employing these Jews in one or the other of their facilities which were dispersed widely around the countryside in the districts of Warsaw, Lublin, Bialostok, and Vilnius.

Getter herself conforms closely to the profile that Nechama Tec has drawn of the Polish Righteous Gentile: devoutly Catholic, socially prominent, highly nationalistic, and intellectual.[16] As a director and founder of orphanages and a superior of her organization, Getter was well known in public circles. Well before the beginning of the war and the Holocaust Getter's work had brought her recognition:

---

15. House archives; letter of Janina Dawidowicz to Sister Olszewska; London, Jan. 11, 1975.

16. Tec, chapter 4.

the Order of the Restored Poland in 1925, and a further distinction in 1931, her country's Gold Cross of Merit.

By the time of Hitler's invasion of Poland in the fall of 1939, Getter had achieved a long record of public service in education and social work. This did not keep her at age 70 from throwing herself into the new work made necessary by the Holocaust. During the wartime German occupation of Poland Getter opened 13 additional homes for children.

No one ordered or told Getter and the sisters of the Family to save Jews. They acted entirely on their own. In 1986 the Holocaust Martyrs and Heroes Remembrance Authority recognized Mother Matylda Getter and the sisters of the Family of Mary as Righteous Gentiles. One tree was planted at the Yad Vashem Holocaust memorial in Jerusalem for Getter and one for all of the rest of the sisters of the Family.[17]

---

17. Earlier, in 1978, another sister of the family, Olga Schwarz, superior of the house in Chelmska was honored by Yad Vashem.

Chapter Two

A Nazi Foe and Catholic Agitator

DURING THE DESPERATE YEARS WHEN GERMANY'S JEWS faced emigration, deportation, and mass murder, Margarete Sommer was in charge of a Berlin church office whose sole purpose was to help them. In this capacity Sommer became acquainted with the ordeal that German Jews faced.

After the collapse of Germany in 1945, Sommer, an intense person, continued to help the remnant of Jews who survived the Holocaust and returned to Berlin. Her work amounted to a 15 year commitment. Religious faith and professionalism as a social worker were the twin pillars that supported Sommer's dedication during these desolate years.

As Berlin's Jews became more despondent with each passing year leading up to the Holocaust, the demands on Sommer's social work became greater and greater. But her faith drove her to try to expand her influence beyond the city of Berlin to the whole country. Her historical significance lies in the fact that she used her Berlin experiences to try to influence the entire German Catholic church to intervene on behalf of Jews.

By the time the National Socialists came to power Sommer had already taken her doctorate in social work at the famous Humboldt University of Berlin. She then found employment with the Prussian state welfare office. Wasting no time, the Nazis fired Sommer in 1934. She then took what turned out to be a lifetime position with the Berlin diocese, initially as a specialist for women's affairs.

It was in this capacity that Sommer first began to combat Nazi racist policy. When Hitler's personnel from the Reich Enterprise for Health and Welfare Facilities (*Reichsarbeitsgemeinschaft für Heil-und Pflegeanstalten*, or, in Nazi jargon, "T-4") called upon a Catholic home for the handicapped in search of potential euthanasia victims, an emergency situation arose. Sommer sought out social workers for Catholic homes and hospitals who could be counted on to protect the physically or mentally disadvantaged children whose lives were endangered.

Before actually being killed, euthanasia victims were transferred from one part of the country to another. This reduced the possibility of interference on the part of relatives. In this situation Catholic hospitals and homes for the mentally handicapped had to depend on their staffs to protect their patients. Protecting the disadvantaged from "T-4," either by falsifying records or by physically hiding people, meant that Sommer and other Catholic women were obstructing Nazi racism.[1]

Sommer had a ringside seat in Berlin to observe Nazi racist policy grow and unfold. During the heated political campaigns of 1931-32, she saw how members of Hitler's party smashed and looted Jewish owned stores on the Kurfürstendamm boulevard, and then, when Hitler took office, how Jews were beaten or roughed up by SA rowdies during their delirious celebration. Next came organized oppression: the national boycott of Jewish businesses and the April Laws of 1933. The second half of the decade brought grim persecution of Jews: the Nuremberg laws (Law for the Protection of German Blood and German

---

1. Bistumsarchiv Berlin (henceforth BAB) Sommer Nachlass; see *Lebenslauf* and correspondence with Zentrale des Katholischen Fürsorgevereins für Mädchen, Frauen und Kinder.

Honor and the Reich Citizen Law) followed by a legal definition of Jewishness, economic exploitation, social isolation and expulsion from Germany.

All of this culminated in a public terrorization of Jews in November of 1938 called the Night of Broken Glass.[2] Jews were roused from sleep, beaten, incarcerated, and occasionally even murdered. Jewish businesses all over the country were smashed and looted, and hundreds of synagogues were desecrated and burned down in nearly every German city of some size.

Although no bishop spoke out to condemn the events of the Night of Broken Glass, it marked the beginning of the Berlin resistance circle. Inspired by the cathedral priest, Bernhard Lichtenberg, whose daily prayers for Germany's persecuted Jews began after the Night of Broken Glass, Sommer became increasingly involved in work on behalf of Jews. Bishop Konrad Preysing appointed Lichtenberg to oversee a new diocesan bureau whose name, the Berlin Office of Special Relief, gave no hint of its purpose of assisting Jews. Sommer began devoting most of her energies toward Special Relief and, when Lichtenberg was arrested and jailed by the Nazis, Preysing asked Sommer to become its director in 1941.[3] In this capacity Sommer began to help Jews who had converted to Catholicism but ended up helping all Jews.

Helping Berlin Jews during the Holocaust

Because the ultimate destiny of European Jews was so terrifying, it is easy to overlook the many smaller difficul-

---

2. Nazis coined the serene and agreeable sounding word 'Kristallnacht' to refer to the frightful events of the second week of November.

3. BAB Sommer Nachlass "Uebersicht über meine Tätigkeit." In this post war "vita" Sommer says that she took over the Special Relief office in 1939; it may be that in effect she directed it since then, but she was not actually appointed director until 1941.

ties and dilemmas that Nazi racist policy caused before the Holocaust itself took place. These problems, so insignificant in comparison with death camp experiences, were real enough to those persecuted and to courageous Gentiles like Sommer. Because she had the courage to confront each issue as it arose, Sommer was drawn closer and closer to resistance as the National Socialist persecution of the Jews grew ever more extreme.

For a dedicated social worker and convinced Christian Berlin offered endless challenges. The city counted 190,000 Jewish citizens in 1936 of whom about 40,000 had converted to Christianity. (It is important to remember that the Nazis considered these people to be Jews regardless of their baptism.) Social complications caused by Nazi racism proliferated within a population of this size. Problems included broken marriages, orphaned children, destitute and isolated elderly Jews, unemployment, and relations between Jewish converts and other Christians.

After the Night of Broken Glass many Jews made up their minds to leave Germany. Often children were the first priority for parents who sought visas for them before looking after themselves. Increasingly after 1938 parents of children who were classified by the regime as *Mischling* (part Jewish) applied to Special Relief to find homes for them outside Germany. In 1939 about one of every four of the approximately 1,000 applications for emigration was a child. Sommer devoted much of her time and Special Relief's resources to this effort.

Sommer worked to obtain emigration papers from the German government and visas from host countries in Europe.[4] Unfortunately, this usually meant France or Holland. Those who emigrated to these countries found them-

---

4. BAB Sommer Nachlass "Kurzer Bericht ü. Entstehung und Entwicklung des Hilfswerks beim Bischöflichen Ordinariat Berlin" (henceforth, "Kurzer Bericht"); this statement was drawn up by Sommer in 1946.

selves trapped in the Nazi web a second time due to German successes during the first years of World War II. It fell then to Sommer to try to resettle these people once again (usually in Brazil).

Between 1934 and 1939 about 2,000 persons classified as Jewish by the Nazis succeeded in getting emigration and visa papers through the church. Roughly 20 percent of these Germans were Berliners. The numbers may strike us as relatively low but they must be understood in the context of the difficulties involved in securing passports and visas. Nationally church agencies dealt with almost 100,000 applicants before placing only 2,000 people. As a result of her close involvement in this work, Margarete Sommer came to know most of the Berlin applicants – not just those who were successful – personally and sometimes intimately.

Finding funds for this work was a problem. In a span of five years the church in Germany spent 360,000RM (about $90,000) for emigration. Roughly half of Special Relief's funds went for this purpose, even though the needs of the huge majority of Berlin Jews who were not able to emigrate grew steadily greater. The National Socialist regime did not allow public fund drives that would benefit Jews, nor did it allow funds collected by Caritas to be used on their behalf. This meant that records had to be juggled, and money "laundered" so that funds could be put at Sommer's disposal.

Catholic and Jewish agencies worked together to help Jews and converted Jews emigrate. The case of Alfred Fabian illustrates this. Fabian was held in a detention camp in 1939, but could be released if funds to travel to Shanghai, China, for which he held a visa, could be found. His expenses ended up being shared by the Jewish Community (840RM), Caritas (200RM), and Special Relief (sum not known). Cases like Fabian's seem to have been common.

When a Jewish convert applied for emigration assistance a record was kept on the date of his or her conversion. Evidently, this was to discourage conversion for the sole purpose of improving one's chances of emigrating. But as the situation of Jews became more and more desperate, Sommer recognized that this would have amounted to an absurdity.

Even though the Special Relief office was set up to help converted Jews, confessional conformity was not a requirement for Sommer. A study of her notebook shows that about 20 percent of those whose emigration she assisted were non-Christian Jews, and that an additional 20 percent were Jewish converts to Protestantism.[5] Because she did not discriminate, Sommer's work on behalf of German Jews won recognition within the Jewish community.[6]

The objectives of Sommer's Special Relief office were much broader than emigration assistance. Sommer attempted to provide moral support and welfare assistance of every sort for Jews. This ranged from supporting elderly people (about 37 percent of all adult clients), the sick and the handicapped, to providing for those who were too indigent to provide for their basic housing and nutritional needs.

Originally, Sommer's clientele consisted of converted Jews, since the Reich Association provided this service for others. When Ursula Benningson converted to Catholicism in July, 1939, her parish priest wrote to Special Relief to say that she should be given assistance (meaning, evidently, that her conversion was sincere). But, as the situation of Berlin Jews became more and more hopeless, confessional preference lost importance. Almost half of the

---

5. BAB Sommer Nachlass See her notebook.
6. BAB 1-100 Richter to Luckner, n.p. (copy), 27 July, 1948.

men who received assistance from Special Relief in 1939-1940 were non-Christian Jews.

After the war began to take its toll in terms of battle fatalities and Jews were deported from Berlin in increasing numbers to concentration camps, Special Relief was faced with a new problem: orphaned children. A *Mischling* child, whose father was killed in the war and whose mother was killed by the Nazis, was helpless. Special Relief sought to care for these children until it could place them in homes. This work took place relatively late in the war, and details on the number of these tragic cases are not available.

The various kinds of welfare work which Special Relief carried on were costly. In a five month period between August of 1939 and February of 1940 the office spent about 5,000RM (roughly $1200) on welfare, which was 1,000RM more than it spent on emigration.[7] It is not clear how the office decided to distribute its limited funds. A decision to dedicate the entire budget to emigration work never seems to have occurred to Sommer. By the time she learned that the government intended a systematic genocide, emigration was no longer possible because of the war.

During World War II when National Socialist policy changed from driving Jews out of Germany to deporting them to ghettos in eastern Europe, and then finally to genocide, Sommer's work took on a new character. She sought to provide last minute assistance for Jews who were about to be "transported," and to look after their needs after they had been "resettled."[8] To accomplish this Special Relief formed parish support groups. The people who took

---

7. BAB Sommer Nachlass See budget statement of 7 Feb., 1940.

8. I have put the words "transported" and "resettled" in quotes to indicate their ambiguous meaning. To the Nazis the words meant transportation to or resettlement in eastern Europe, but in 1942 it meant transportation to one of the six death camps and, usually, the immediate demise of the victims. For Jews the words conveyed something dreadful and, increasingly, something morbid.

part in this work involved themselves in serious civil disobedience when they hid Jews who were trying to avoid the fate of deportation to a ghetto in eastern Europe or of the concentration camp.

To understand how Sommer was able to organize this work, let us briefly review the frightful process of "transporting" people. Although occasionally a terrifying *razzia* took place, such as that of February 27, 1943 in Berlin, deportations were normally individual rather than collective.[9] A family was simply notified that the time of its "transportation" had come, although the exact moment of the forced evacuation from house and home was withheld. Now however long a person or family might have anticipated final notification, its arrival often caused unimaginable despair, hopelessness, and trauma. As a rule there were only a few hours between the time of notification and the moment of actual departure from home. Mentally paralyzed, many people simply could not function during these fearful hours of uncertainty. Many were incapable of thinking about the immediate necessities that would be of some practical use during the forced journey that awaited them.

Sommer wanted to help these victims through the moment of crisis. She organized groups of parish volunteers, presumably people who knew the unfortunate deportees, who stood ready so that one or two could go to a family's home at a moment's notice. Once there they attempted to prepare the person, "who in his bewilderment had lost all sensible orientation," for the imminent ordeal of "transportation." The visitors helped with packing and took care of last minute household details. Mostly, of course, they attempted to comfort the persons about to be caught up in National Socialism's ghettoization or death

---

9. For an account of Berlin and its Jewish citizens during the Holocaust, see Leonard Gross, *The Last Jews in Berlin* (New York, 1982).

camp operation. At some point a coded telephone message was made to the parish priest, who came to expend the sacraments of penance and the eucharist.

The scene conjured up by these last minute visits may strike us as more grotesque than humane. Just what does one say to a person facing permanent departure from hearth and home for life or death in a concentration camp? There were, however, several circumstances which cast a softer light on the mission and which may help us understand it better. First, it appears that one of the visitors was herself of Jewish origin. All of the personnel of Special Relief with the single exception of Margarete Sommer were Jewish converts. This could have a double significance. Since the person whose "transportation" was imminent was often Christian, he or she would be given solace by a woman whose religious background was similar or identical. More importantly, the person offering solace faced exactly the same destiny, deportation, as the person whose imminent departure had occasioned her visit. Their common destiny undoubtedly made the compassion of the farewell mission genuine, allowing comforter and victim to bond in mutual support.

In addition, the victim was assured continuing assistance on the part of a support group from his or her parish. To this end circular letters made the rounds of Berlin parishes so that Catholics who knew or recognized the names of those being "transported" could provide continued support by contributing food or dry goods for their use. Packages were sent to Warsaw, Theresienstadt, and Lodz where most Berliners were ghettoized.[10]

Finally, it was most reassuring for victims to know that if they were able to survive whatever ordeal lay ahead, and return one day to Germany, they could go "home." In

---

10. BAB Sommer Nachlass "Kurzer Bericht."

other words, those who remained behind promised to keep track of the property of the deported. Restitution was, in fact, an ongoing work of the Special Relief office during the years immediately following the war.

Since relief was organized by the Berlin diocese and carried out through its parishes, it might appear that Catholics were involved only with Catholics. Such was not the case. Sommer was explicit on this point, saying in her brief postwar memoir that aid was extended to all Jews. It is clear from other records that the National Socialist persecution of the Jews created a common bond among them that cut through lines of religious preference.

Whether Christian or non-Christian, Jews pondered the meaning of the experience which gripped them. Thus, Gertrud Jaffe, a convert to Catholicism, worked in the missions of the Special Relief office to help as many as she could irrespective of their religious preference, and then decided, with great inner resolve, to give herself up for deportation and certain death in order to identify, as a Christian, with the suffering of her people.[11] It worked the other way as well. Jews who were not Christian, like Dr. Martha Mosse, worked to help and save other Jews regardless of their religion.[12]

Although Special Relief and parish support groups attempted to comfort Jews about to be "transported," there were few illusions as time went on as to what fate awaited them. By the beginning of 1942 Sommer had detailed information about life in the ghettos to which Berlin Jews were being herded: 30 to 80 people inhabiting one room; no heating; no plumbing, and four small slices of bread for

---

11. BAB Sommer Nachlass "Zum Gedächtniss on Frau Jaffe." This was written by her parish priest.
12. BAB Sommer Nachlass See Sommer's "To Whom It May Concern Letter" on Martha Mosse, Berlin, 6 June, 1947.

a day's rations.[13] In all likelihood Sommer knew of systematic murder before the end of the year.

At some point, certainly no later than the end of 1942, the Special Relief office began hiding Jews. There are a number of explicit references in Sommer's papers that establish this activity, yet it is difficult to piece together the story of how this was accomplished. Because of constant Gestapo surveillance and the great risk involved, Sommer and the other personnel of Special Relief preferred not to deal by letter or even by telephone, but by personal contact. Obviously, no systematic records would have been kept.

As an additional precaution against divulging information under duress to the Gestapo, no one was told or wanted to know what she did not need to know. Not even Sommer knew how many Jews were being hidden by Special Relief personnel or by parish support groups working with them, because, as she says in her postwar memoir, it was a secret.

Still, Sommer knew some particulars. When one of her coworkers at the Special Relief office, Lieselotte Neumark, faced deportation, she went into hiding with a gentile family. After four weeks Neumark contacted Sommer through a third party to arrange a meeting. Not wishing to endanger any longer the family with whom she was hiding, Neumark asked Sommer to help her sneak onto the next "transport."[14] Sommer was also aware that yet another Special Relief employee, *Fräulein* Joachim, helped ill Jews and hidden Jews "at great personal risk" throughout the period of National Socialist persecution.[15]

---

13. Veröffentlichungen der Kommission für Zeitgeschichte (henceforth VKZ) Reihe A, Vol. 34, 675-78; Bericht Sommers, Berlin, 14 Feb., 1942.

14. BAB Sommer Nachlass Sommer to Anneliese Triller, Berlin, 11 Sept., 1946. Neumark did not survive the war.

15. BAB Sommer Nachlass See Sommer's letter on Joachim, Berlin, 9 July, 1946.

Hiding Jews involved more than just a single person or family risking itself. A support team had to be arranged. This was necessary because of food rationing. As the fortunes of war turned against Germany, staples were rationed. That meant that several families would have to share a small portion of their rations to support the family hiding the Jewish refugee. Support groups were also necessary because of Gestapo surveillance and house searches. If a family came to realize it was being watched, or if it was tipped off that the Gestapo intended to search its home, the refugee had to be temporarily moved to another place. Obviously, this would also be necessary if the host family had to be away from home for a period of time.

Lawrence Baron has estimated that 5,000 Jews were in hiding in Berlin at one time of whom about 1000 survived.[16] Clearly, a large number of Berliners were hiding Jews during the Holocaust. We also know that some of the rescuers were in touch with one another by word of mouth. What we do not know is to what extent these various individuals or teams were networking with each other.

Through her work in Berlin, Sommer became sensitive to the burdens that Nazism had placed on the entire Jewish population. Her familiarity with the victims was immediate and personal. She knew about the family circumstances of the victims – whether they were married to a gentile Catholic, the relationship between spouses one of whom was Jewish or part Jewish, the religious preference of the children. When survivors of the Holocaust drifted back to Berlin after the war or emerged from hiding places, Sommer could testify to the details of the persecution that they had been through. "The difficulty of this work," Sommer wrote after several years experience, "lies in the fact that

---

16. See his essay "The Historical Context of Rescue" in Samuel P. and Pearl M. Oliner, *The Altruistic Personality. Rescuers of Jews in Nazi Europe.* New York: Free Press, 1988, 24.

those affected (by National Socialist antisemitism) are psy-
chologically deeply depressed because of the hopelessness
of the efforts (to help them)."[17] We may infer from these
words that Sommer also found her work to be depressing.

A further strain on Sommer resulted from the fact that
those Jews who had become converted felt that the church
did not care enough about them in their plight. Sommer
shared this opinion. It was clearly her personal involvement with Berlin Jewry and her sensitivity to their predicament that led her to try to raise the awareness of the entire
church to the desperateness of the situation.

Sommer and the Catholic Church during the Holocaust

During the war years Sommer's work on behalf of Jews
spread from the city of Berlin to the entire country. This
first happened in the fall of 1941 when Jews were obliged
to wear the Star of David in public. This meant, of course,
that Catholics would worship at services along side of
converts wearing the star. This situation seems to have
caused greater turmoil among Protestants than Catholics,
but it was also a matter of concern to the latter, and especially to Margarete Sommer. Evidently, some Catholics refused to kneel next to a converted Jew to take the eucharist
at the communion rail, and some priests began avoiding
Jews after the September 1941 Star of David decree.[18]

Because of her position within the diocese and, no
doubt, because of Bishop Preysing's support, Sommer
could address this issue "officially." Thus, we find Sommer
writing to the dean of the German Catholic episcopacy,

---

17. BAB Nachlass Sommer See Sommer's 1938 paper marked "Streng Ver-
traulich" entitled "Die Tätigkeit des Hilfsausschusses für den katholischen Nichtarier im Jahre 1938."

18. VKZ Reihe A, Vol. 34, 550-551; this report is at odds with the report of
Bishop Berning to Cardinal Bertram, Osnabrück, 27 Oct., 1941, in *ibid.*,
583-84.

Cardinal Bertram, offering advice on how the church should deal with this matter. She warned that any prejudicial action, such as instituting separate services for Catholic Jews, would be an additional psychological burden for them at a time when they were already being tormented.

Sommer did not exaggerate. The diary of Erma Becker-Cohen demonstrates how painfully some baptized Jews felt the betrayal of "aryan" Christians who rejected them after the Star decree.[19] Sommer advised that bishops should awaken the consciences of priests and lay people with regard to the Jewish predicament and urge them on to a truly catholic community which lives in the spirit of charity.

The response of the church was disappointing and, in part, disturbing. Priests were instructed to avoid any announcements that would be embarrassing for Jewish Catholics, such as declaring a portion of the communion rail off-limits for them. Special Sunday services for Jews only were to be avoided but when and if Jewish Catholics inquired about this, they were to be advised to go to the earliest possible Mass. Parish priests were advised not to bring this matter up, unless there was unrest among the faithful, in which case they were to be admonished in the spirit of St. Paul to have charity toward all.

But, on the other hand, Jews were to be advised to attend separate services in the event that gentile Catholics, such as bureaucrats or members of the National Socialist party, made a scene by leaving the church during services to protest the presence of Jews. Cardinal Bertram's letter to the country's Catholic bishops, in which these directives were spelled out, concluded with a reminder from St. Paul that in Christ there is neither Jew nor Greek. But there was clearly "Jew and National Socialist party member" and, if

---

19. Claudia Koonz, *Mothers in the Fatherland*. New York: St. Martin's Press, 1986, pp. 15-16.

it should come down to it, the former would be sacrificed in the interests of the latter.[20]

In the end it appears that "aryan" Catholics prayed along side of Jewish converts without much ado. An absence of further directives about this situation is an indication that the matter never became a big problem. Since many converted Jews lived in Berlin itself, Sommer would have been able to deal more directly with problems if they arose there.

During the war years Sommer played a key role in warding off another National Socialist attack on Jews – the dissolution of all Jewish-Gentile marriages. There was nothing the church could do, of course, if an "aryan" Catholic wanted to be rid of his or her Jewish spouse. A person needed only to apply to a court, and a divorce was immediately granted. Thus, Werner Borcher divorced Stella, who was raised a Catholic although both her parents were Jewish, in February, 1940. Werner provided very little money for the support of his children, before dropping out of sight altogether in 1943. As a Jewess Stella found it difficult to find work that would pay enough to support her family. Having to wear the Star of David distressed her because of her fear that it would lead directly to deportation. After a time, she ceased wearing it, but then had to fear the consequences from the Gestapo if she was found out. Such cases cut Sommer to the quick. Unfortunately, the Borcher divorce case was not uncommon. It reflected, in Sommer's opinion, "the arrogance of the aryan spouse" which "in most cases is the reason for the subsequent misery of the non-aryan party."[21] Women in Stella Borcher's position

---

20. The absence of subsequent material on this question in volumn 34 of VKZ may be an indication that the presence of Jewish Catholics at church services did not become a problem; Bishop Berning of Osnabrilck said as much. In *Mothers in the Fatherland*, Koonz gives the opposite impression; see pages 16-17.

found it next to impossible to provide for their children. Many turned to the Special Relief office for child support assistance. Thus, when Sommer learned of the plan to dissolve all Jewish-Gentile marriages, she was well aware of what the impact on individuals and families would be.

The proposed decree, barbarous in its terms, presented Sommer with a springboard to appeal for action on the part of the entire church. Through their apparently numerous contacts within the administration and party, Sommer and her associates learned of the terms of the imminent decree.[22] Gentile spouses were to divorce their Jewish partners in the immediate future or their marriages would be declared dissolved by the state. A child of such a marriage could declare loyalty to either parent – if for the Jew, the future meant deportation; if for the Gentile, life in Germany as a sterilized, publicly identified *Mischling*.

Working with Bishop Preysing, Sommer acted quickly to ward off the declaration on divorce. In November she wrote a strong letter to Cardinal Bertram in which she emphasized the violation of church law and the human tragedy that would ensue. It appears that the decree was enacted prematurely in certain areas in the city of Berlin, because Sommer was able to provide Bertram with concrete examples of the distress the decree would cause. In one case, an entire family committed suicide. Sommer pointed out that there were thousands of cases of sacramental marriages in Germany between Catholic Gentiles and Jews.

---

21. BAB I/1-99 Sommer to H. Galinsky, n.p. (copy), Aug. 8, 1948.

22. Sommer and the Berlin circle of Catholic resistors were in constant touch with Heinrich Grüber who stated during the Eichmann trial that he had many contacts within the party and administration; see H.D. Leuner, *When Compassion Was a Crime* (London, 1966), 114-119. Sommer also would have known about Kurt Gerstein's account of the process of genocide going on in Poland; see Saul Friedländer, *Counterfeit Nazi* (London, 1969), 158.

Would the bishops allow the state to "put asunder what God had joined together?"

Sommer went so far as to urge the bishops to ask Pope Pius XII to intervene by writing personally to Hitler. Thus, the proposed decree gave Sommer an excellent emotional and doctrinal issue with which to urge the hierarchy to act.

The reaction of the Catholic church to this crisis was much more resolute than was the case with the presence of converted Jews at Mass. A protest from Cardinal Bertram, together with planned, simultaneous local protests on the part of both Protestant and Catholic churches, forestalled the divorce decree.[23]

Thwarted in this direct attack on Jewish-Gentile marriages, the Nazi regime began dealing with the "problem" through police action early in 1943. On the last Saturday of February the operation code named *Aktion Fabrik* took place in Berlin. Without warning 8,000 Jews were taken directly from their work stations to temporary, make-shift detention facilities, and then within 24 to 48 hours evacuated to concentration camps or ghettos in eastern Europe. Among those who were deported were many Christian Jews who had married gentile Christians.

Margarete Sommer, after having witnessed the great Berlin roundup, set off immediately for Breslau, where she reported the details of the deportation to Cardinal Bertram. On the second and third of March, Bertram dispatched a strong protest to top National Socialist administrators, including Goebbels.

The events of late February established a pattern of action and reaction on the part of the regime and the church. By April the bishops had worked out a coordinated, nation-wide response should the divorce decree be pro-

---

23. Erich Klausener, "Margarete Sommer," *Miterbauer des Bistums Berlin*, ed. Wolfgang Knauft (Berlin, 1979), 175; VKZ Reihe A, Vol. 38, 21.

claimed. Probably because of this threat, the regime continued to violate the sacramentality of Jewish-Gentile marriages by simply deporting the "non-aryan" party. During the summer months, Sommer was in frequent contact with a number of bishops, keeping them abreast of the persecution of Jews. Her familiarity with the problems confronting the Jewish populace led the bishops to appoint her to draw up reports for them on the situation.

Sommer filed her first report almost immediately. It provided little hope for a change in the regime's conduct. Jews were being arrested and deported on the most frivolous pretexts such as going to an "aryan" barber shop. Temporary detention (before deportation) was under cruel conditions: large rooms divided by chicken-wire into tiny cells of one cot's length and two cots' breadth. In some cases families received word of the deaths of Jewish relatives just 14 days after their deportation. Sommer's information was based on reports from various areas in Germany besides Berlin. "In this way," Sommer concluded, "the administration was dealing with the "mixed" marriage problem in widespread areas of the country."

The bishops' frequent protests, based on Sommer's stream of information, had some temporary effect. In the long run, of course, the protests of the bishops did not deter the National Socialists from "transporting" German Jews.

Although Special Relief and parish support groups attempted to comfort Jews about to be "transported," there were few illusions as to what fate awaited them. After the war, Sommer wrote that she knew "from secret sources of information" that most of the Jews who were deported died soon thereafter.[24] But it is difficult to say how early she knew this. She hints strongly at it in her report to the

---

24. BAB Sommer Nachlass "Kurzer Bericht." One of Sommer's sources of information seems to have been Bernhard Lösener of Nürnberg Law fame.

bishops on the great *razzia* in Berlin early in 1943 when 8,000 Jews were "very cruelly rounded up and literally driven" into trucks. Explaining that authorities would not allow the families of the detained Jews to bring them provisions for the imminent "transportation," Sommer concluded that "precisely this circumstance . . . changed our suspicion into a certainty that they had no future."[25]

What we know about the clandestine operation of the Special Relief office is regrettably little. But the important thing is for us to be aware of the fact of their involvement in rescue work. A few Catholics crossed the line of civil disobedience. They resisted Hitler. They hid Jews.

But Sommer was not able to coax her church's bishops over this line into open conflict with National Socialism and resistance against Hitler's regime. She was obviously in a position to to do this, having become the episcopacy's consultant on Jewish affairs.

Situated as she was in Berlin, Sommer had an entire network of contacts through which she learned of the Holocaust even as it was unfolding. The list is stunning: Heinrich Grüber, who later stated that he had many informants within the party and administration;[26] SS officer Kurt Gerstein, who informed an associate of Sommer in August, 1942, about genocide in Poland;[27] a few months later another associate, the Munich Jesuit Augustin Rösch, learned that the plan to deport and exterminate Jews "is frequently already underway";[28] above all, Sommer was in regular – sometimes daily – contact with Hans Globke, a high level

---

25. VKZ Reihe A, Vol. 38, 19-21; Bericht Sommer, Berlin, 2 March, 1943.

26. Leuner, *When Compassion Was a Crime*, 114-119.

27. *Rundbrief zur Förderung der Freundschaft zwischen dem alten und dem neuen Gottesvolk – im Geiste der beiden Testamente*, xxx, nos. 113-116 (1978), 129-135.

28. Augustin Rösch, Kampf Gegen den Nationalsozialismus, ed. Roman Bleistein (Frankfurt: Knecht, 1985), 206.

bureaucrat in the Interior Ministry who later became a witness for the prosecution at the Nuremberg trials.[29] In all probability, Globke was the "secret source of information" that Sommer spoke of after the war.

Sommer made it her business to make sure that Cardinal Bertram knew about the atrocities that Germans were perpetrating against Jews, including German Jews, in eastern Europe. Since the German bishops spoke with one voice, Bertram had to be won over if a strong statement of protest was to be forthcoming. Not all of Sommer's reports to Bertram appear to be extant, but, judging from those that are, we can say that she was both timely and accurate.[30] About the Kovno massacre (October 27, 1941), which included Jews from Berlin and elsewhere in Germany, Sommer reported that

> . . . the Jews must undress (it could have been 18 degrees below freezing), then climb into "graves" previously dug by Russian prisoners of war. They were then shot with a machine gun; then grenades were tossed in. Without checking to see if all were dead, the Kommando ordered the grave filled in.[31]

Thus, just slightly more than three months elapsed since the Kovno massacre until Germany's Catholic bishops and their titular head, Cardinal Bertram, had an accurate account of this atrocity.

In 1943 Sommer reported to Bertram personally on the Berlin roundup, *Aktion Fabrik*, the incident that led her to conclude that the deported Jews would not live long. In August she filed her lengthy report that dealt with the

---

29. See the information on Globke in BAB I/1-103.

30. Sommer's reports are reproduced in volumes 24 and 38 of VKZ Reihe A. The original documents, if they exist, are in Breslau, now part of Poland. The Breslau archival holdings were microfilmed and are now housed in the VKZ archives in Bonn. I am indebted to the director of the archives, Ulrich von Hehl, for letting me use the microfilm.

31. VKZ Reihe A, Vol. 24, 675-78; Sommer's Report 1942.

treatment of Jews from a number of regions in Germany and Austria; this was the report which said that the "aryan" families of those who had been deported received death notices on them 14 days thereafter. At the exact same time Bertram also received an extraordinary letter from a Polish Jew, which provided page after page of accounts of the murder of four million Jews by Germans, and which concluded with the indictment that "every German, yourself included, is guilty of these atrocities."[32] The months that followed brought more reports from Sommer.

Because they knew that Jews were being murdered, Bishop Preysing and Sommer brought pressure on Cardinal Bertram urging him to take the lead in promulgating an official Catholic warning about the genocide. What Preysing and Sommer wanted was a protest statement. Our point of departure, they suggested, must concern Christian Jews and sacramental marriages involving Jews, but our statement "must clearly go beyond that to include the atrocities against Jews in general."[33]

Sommer's draft statement demanded specific rights for the deported Jews, such as healthy living conditions, correspondence privileges, religious services, personal contact with an inspection committee, and so on. Preysing warned his fellow bishops that "we will stand guilty before God and man if we are silent" about Hitler's persecution of Jews.[34]

Instead of winning Bertram over, Sommer's reports had the effect of straining the relationship between him and the Berlin circle of Catholics. Bertram refused to endorse the draft on the grounds that there was insufficient proof of the conditions which it sought to redress. It was,

---

32. *Ibid.,* Vol. 34, 210-215.
33. VKZ Reihe A, Vol. 38, 99-100.
34. VKZ Reihe A, Vol. 38, 220-221.

of course, impossible for Sommer to provide proof without disclosing the identity of those in the regime and administration who leaked information to her. She therefore continued to bring as detailed information as she could to Bertram, invoking the authority of her bishop and confidant, Konrad Preysing, to authenticate her mission.

All of this exasperated Bertram who grew weary of Sommer's persistence. The cardinal finally notified Berlin that in the future Sommer's reports would have to be undersigned by bishop Preysing verifying their details and correctness. "Please make this clear to Frau Dr. Sommer" Bertram wrote, "since my warnings don't help. Otherwise I will not schedule anymore appointments with her."[35]

The effort of Sommer and the Berlin circle to spread resistance through the entire German church failed. Rather than protest, the bishops pleaded faintly. In November, 1942, Cardinal Bertram urged that "other races" be treated humanely, as did the 1943 Fulda Bishops' Letter. Lacking in these pronouncements is the sense of outrage that typified their attitude toward euthanasia. There is no statement from the bishops that addressed the excruciating situation of Jews in the ghettos or of those murdered by machine guns in open pits or in gas chambers.

Sommer's Work with Survivors After the War

When the Allied forces finally brought an end to Hitler and his Nazi regime in 1945, the remnant of the Jewish people who had survived his savagery were in desperate need of care. Sommer dedicated herself to them for the next seven years of her life. Thus, for Sommer the war's end did not

---

35. VKZ, 38, 350, footnote 2; quote is taken from a letter from Bertram to Prange, the Vicar General of the diocese of Berlin, written on April 17, 1944.

mark a new beginning, but a continuation of what she had been about for the previous seven years.

Germany awoke at the end of the war to a "cold, gray dawn."[36] The country had been devastated from within by the Nazis and from without by her enemies. Nowhere was the picture more grim than in Berlin, where the capital and Hitler's underground bunker had drawn wave after wave of Allied bombers. For this reason alone Sommer's postwar work would have been depressing, but other factors, such as dissension among the relief forces and indifference toward Jewish victims, added greatly to her distress. In a certain sense it had been easier to fight against Hitler, a known entity, than it was to struggle against the faceless difficulties of postwar Germany.

For Sommer there was no escape from her mission, simply because so many Holocaust survivors emerged after the war in Berlin. In 1946 Sommer estimated that of the approximately 20,000 German Jewish survivors 13,000 resided in her city. Protestant, Catholic, and Jewish agencies cared for these survivors according to the faith preference of each.

This posed a major problem in itself. Foreign relief agencies just could not grasp the fact that to Hitler and the Nazis it did not matter whether a Jew had converted to Christianity. The number of converts who, like Edith Stein, had perished during the Holocaust numbered in the many thousands. Those who had not perished were just as much in need of support as other survivors of the Holocaust.

In 1946 Sommer was already assisting about 3,000 survivors. This included the 700 who had survived by hiding in Berlin but were now severely undernourished and ill. Children under 14 years of age were under repre-

---

36. Gordon A. Craig, *Germany, 1866-1945* (New York: Oxford U. Press, 1980), 715.

sented in the group, Sommer reported, because "after 1933 Jewish families only occasionally had the courage to bring children into the world."[37]

Caring for these survivors posed a variety of problems of both a material and non-material nature. At a time when there was hardly enough food to maintain the general population at a subsistence level, relief agencies were completely dependent on international aid. But foreign agencies could not remedy the housing problem of bombed out German cities.

At the other end of the process questions arose regarding the recipients. How were those who had been living underground for a number of years to be reliably identified? Which survivors were most deserving of assistance? Who should be employed first? Given housing first? How should the small amount of monetary relief be divided up among survivors?

It may be that Sommer found the nonmaterial problems even more vexing and distressing. She could not understand the attitude of the general German public, including Catholics, which simply did not accept the fact that "these people deserved any consideration at all." It was much easier, Sommer wrote, to enlist support for Jews during the years of Hitler's persecution than after the war. This attitude carried over to Berlin's city administrators who Sommer described as being "small of heart," because of the minimal amount of financial help they funneled to the Victims of Fascism (*Opfer des Faschismus*) organization.

Most devastating of all to Sommer was the infighting among Protestant, Catholic, and Jewish survivor relief agencies. Because Hitler had persecuted Jews indiscriminantly, a solidarity arose among Berlin Jews regardless of

---

37. Material dealing with Sommer's work after the war is preserved the the archives of the diocese of Berlin, files I/1-99, I/1-100, and I/1-103.

religious preference during the Nazi era. This also extended, as we saw, to Sommer who assisted or hid Jews
whether converts or not.[38] After the war Sommer saw this
spirit evaporate.

Because of her wartime work, Sommer was a valuable
resource for the Victims of Fascism committee which cared
for survivors. Her close familiarity with many of the returning survivors' situations allows us to glimpse the impact of Nazi racism on people's lives. Thus, Ursula
Guttstadt, an office worker, had been in ballet training until
the Nuremberg Laws were passed; Yavonne Silbermann
had intended to be a children's doctor until her education
was halted by the Nazis; Peter Granberg, born in 1933, was
orphaned because his "aryan" mother abandoned him after
having divorced her Jewish husband who then died during
the war; Rudolf Hertwig's Jewish father died in a concentration camp and his Christian mother, who lives in
Breslau, pays no attention to him." In Sommer's files there
are dozens of such cases about which she had been con-
sulted by the committee on Victims of Fascism.[39]

It occasionally happened that the committee rejected
the application for assistance of a survivor whose case
Sommer had supported. When such instances arose, Sommer asked the committee to notify her, because, she said,
"in most instances I knew the persecuted people themselves during the years of oppression (and) my testimony
should carry more weight than that of a denouncer whose
motives cannot be verified."[40] Berta Kirchhoff was a case
in point. Sommer had known this woman from 1940 on
and she testified that she had had to wear the Star of David

38. Michael Phayer, *Protestant and Catholic Women in Nazi Germany*, Detroit: Wayne State U. Press, 1990, 216.

39. I/J-gg. Sommer to Herr Bock, Magistrate of the city of Berlin; Member of Main Committee of the Victims of Fascism; n.p., copy; 24 July, 1946.

40. BAB WT-99. Sommer to H. Galinsky, n.p. (copy); Aug. 19, 1948.

and could have been deported. "It makes no matter if she used an illegal "aryan" card to get rations or if she covered up the star; she risked arrest daily and hourly by doing this."

Cases involving divorce frequently arose, and they aroused bitterness in Sommer. Apparently, the Victims of Fascism committee felt it needed to know whether a Jew had converted to Christianity in order to save himself or herself. (There was a window of time when the Nazis respected the sacramentality of marriage by not deporting the Jewish spouse.) This angered Sommer who knew that in most cases a divorce left the Jewish spouse in poverty and in danger. "In this regard I'm very adamant and inflexible" she told the committee.[41]

Sommer became irritated when the Victims of Fascism committee denied assistance to a Jewish convert who had sought and obtained a divorce during the Holocaust. Sometimes, Sommer told the committee, it was only possible to obtain a visa and emigration papers if the Jewish party was single. Later on during the Holocaust, after the Nazis had begun to deport persons of Jewish ancestry even if they were married to Christians, divorces occurred so that the non-Jewish spouse could make arrangements to conceal the former spouse.

Sommer explained to the committee that she knew of cases in which it was only by obtaining a divorce that either the husband or wife could work out an illegal existence for the (former) Jewish spouse and safeguard the person during the time of lawlessness (Hitler era). Sometimes, Sommer said, the non-Jewish spouse was highly reluctant to part with his or her spouse and submitted only after "intensive pleading and urging." Sommer warned the committee that she would raise the "sharpest objections" if it

---

41. BAB I/1-99 Sommer to H. Galinsky, n.p. (copy), Aug. 8, 1948.

denied assistance to a survivor whose divorce had been undertaken with good intentions.

Sommer's postwar work subjected her to considerable stress. The circumstance of great need together with a scarcity of relief funds made this inevitable. But other factors that Sommer faced alone compounded the mental stress. It fell to her, for example, to make out the official church death notices for those converted Jews who did not survive the Holocaust. In the course of her work Sommer had come to know many of these people and their families personally.

Exasperating as well was the attitude of Germans at large toward survivors. Sommer found it continually astonishing that "no one can understand why anything needs to be done on behalf of these people" (survivors).[42] Germans had already forgotten the "awful persecution of the Jews, the destruction of their homes, their ghettoization, and their outright murder."[43] Catholics, Sommer noticed, suffered from this callousness. As a result there was no one with whom Sommer could commiserate or even discuss this problem.

Under these circumstances it was impossible for the German "righteous Gentile" like Sommer to speak out. Others would accuse them of self-serving adulation and of promoting themselves at the expense of fellow countrymen.

The postwar years were then for Sommer "a cold gray dawn" just as they were for other Germans, but for different reasons. Sommer's stress expressed itself in the way she lashed out at those with whom she worked on behalf of survivors and for whom, in reality, she had great respect. Thus, she referred to Pastor Grüber as a dictator and dis-

---

42. BAB I/1-99 Sommer to Ludger Born, SJ; n.p. (copy); Feb. 21, 1948.
43. BAB I/1-99 Sommer to Berlin Caritasdirektor Albs, Berlin-Dahlem; 24 July, 1952.

paraged Luckner's efforts in considerable detail to a mutual friend. The pressure of the work eased considerably when the State of Israel became a reality in 1948, making emigration on a large scale possible for survivors. Yet, for those who chose to stay on indemnification by the German government was inexcusably delayed.

In 1954 the Special Relief office, which had assisted so many Jews over a dozen years, was closed. Sommer's work at that point became more diversified, but her experiences during the Nazi years preoccupied her mentally for the rest of her life, tormenting her and keeping her from peace of mind. The postwar climate in Germany was such that people who had resisted the Nazi persecution of the Jews could not speak their minds in righteous anger without courting public disfavor.[44]

This circumstance was compounded because Sommer was a strong Catholic living in an era and religious culture which deprived women of authority. Sommer could not bring herself to speak out against her church, faulting it for its failure to confront Hitler over the Holocaust.

Unable to blame others, Margarete Sommer, who had done more for Jews during the Holocaust than most of her countrymen, blamed herself for not having done more. The torment of the Jews became her torment until her death in 1965 at 72 years of age.

---

44. It is true that Sommer's heroism was recognized when she was awarded a Cross of Honor but this did not occur for more than a decade after the war.

Chapter Three

Margit Slachta's Efforts to Rescue Central European Jews, 1939-1945

APRIL 2, 1942 MARKED THE ZENITH OF DEPORTATIONS OF JEWS by the Slovakian government. On that day Margit Slachta wrote to the Bishop of Kalosca, "My conscience tells me that I am an accomplice when I have not tried to do everything in my power to put an end to these acts."[1] Her words capture the essence of her work for Central European Jews between 1939 and 1945. With her colleagues and a few other Roman Catholic supporters, Slachta protested through letters, confronted government authorities, petitioned church officials, and organized hostels and hiding places for Jews traveling through Hungary and Slovakia while trying to escape Nazi persecution.[2]

Margit Slachta was born in Kassa, Hungary (now known as Kosice in Slovakia) in 1884. Early in life she emigrated to the United States with her parents where they lived for a short period. She earned a secondary education degree in German and French languages from a Catholic training school in Budapest. There she met Carlotta Koranyi, a Hungarian, who inspired her to defend the rights of working

---

1. Margit Slachta's letter to Bishop of Kalocsa, April 27, 1942. Mária Schmidt, "Margit Slachta's Activities in Support of Slovakian Jewry, 1942-1943" *Remembering for the Future.* Vol. I, Jews and Christians During and After the Holocaust. New York: Pergamon Press, 1988, 208.

2. "Sister Margaret Slachta Dies; Champion of Rights," *Buffalo Evening News,* January 7, 1974; "Sister Margaret Slachta, Founded Order in Hungary," *New York Times,* January 8, 1974, 36:3.

women. She later met Koranyi in Berlin where she went to study the problems of working women. While there she also learned how to organize individuals for "collective action." Slachta's political consciousness heightened as she grew aware of the need to promote political rights for women. When she returned to Hungary, she formed several Catholic women's organizations that would later aid her in rescue efforts.[3] After World War I, Slachta headed the Union of Catholic Women, which was transformed into an independent political caucus known as the Party of Christian Women. In 1920-1921 Slachta became the first woman elected to the Hungarian Parliament where she focused attention on the condition of women and children.

In 1908, when Edith Farkas formed the Society of the Social Mission, Slachta was among the first to join the community and to profess its spiritual values.[4] Later she began a new community which grew under her leadership to become the Society of the Sisters of Social Service in 1923. Slachta opened the first motherhouse in Budapest.[5] The Society had an "apostolic nature" and required members to live in common and pursue a life dedicated to charity in everyday life.[6] Slachta viewed her community

---

3. Sister Natalie Palagyi, Sister of Social Service, letter to author, January 5, 1994; Margit Slachta was Sister Natalie Palagyi's formation director and Sister Palagyi has provided many first hand accounts for this research. G. Rocca, *Dizionario degli istituti de perfezione*, trans. by J.P. Donnelly, vol. 8, col. 1554.

4. "Some Early History," Sisters of Social Service Newsletter, Spring-Summer 1991, No. 11 Archives of Sisters of Social Service, Buffalo, NY (hereafter cited as SSSA).

5. The clerical president of the Sisters of Social Service was Bishop Count Janos Mikes (1923-1948). It was under Slachta's leadership that the Society established itself in five countries providing qualified social workers to women and children. Mária Schmidt, "Action of Margit Slachta to Rescue Slovakian Jews." *Danubian Historical Studies*, 1 (Spring 1987) 58; G. Rocca, col. 1434-1435.

6. Margit Slachta, *From the Hermitage of the Desert to the Center of Life.* (Budapest, c. 1940), SSSA.

as one designed to meet contemporary problems and those of the future through social work among the poor.[7] The Sisters of Social Service served women and children without regard to creed or ethnicity. During World War II, Slachta coupled her religious convictions with political activities and worked as an advocate for Jews. This advocacy infused her articles, letters, and spiritual writings. Self-confident and strong, she relied on the assistance of her sisters and of Hungarian women in high places to accomplish her objectives.[8] Margit Slachta's story highlights important contributions that an individual can make in contrast to the slow moving bureaucracies of large institutions such as the state and church.

Europe 1940 – The Voice of the Spirit

Adolph Hitler invaded Poland on September 1, 1939. He then made it clear that he would impose "strict measures" to regulate the "Jewish problem" within the Greater Reich. This dictum acted as a catalyst for the eastward migration of Jewish families who fell under the immediate threat of the German army. Hungary's territorial acquisitions, which had resulted from a favorable relationship with Hitler during the late 1930s, aggravated Jewish dislocation.[9] The Hun-

---

7. There is a clear distinction between "sisters who live in a house" and "nuns who live in a convent." The Sisters of Social Service, according to canonical law, are similar to the Daughters of Charity of Saint Vincent de Paul who take annual vows, live in open community houses, and serve in the secular world. James A. Coriden, Thomas J. Green, and Donald E. Heintschel. *The Code of Canon Law.* New York: Paulist Press, 1994, 535.

8. Margit Slachta's letters were compiled and translated by Tamàs Majsai, "The Deportation of Jews from Csíkszereda and Margit Slachta's Intervention on their Behalf." *Studies in the Holocaust in Hungary,* ed. Randolph Braham. New York: Columbia University Press, 1990, 114-117.

9. The basic history of the Holocaust in Hungary is provided by Randolph Braham, *The Politics of Genocide: The Holocaust in Hungary,* vols. I & II, New York: Columbia University Press, 1994.

garian government appointed Miklós Kozma, Commissioner for Carpatho-Ruthenia, the territory acquired from Czechoslovakia in 1939, to oversee the removal of Jews. Initially, Slachta had heard about attacks on Jews from the Transylvanian branch of the Social Sisterhood. She responded to their letters seeking support and began to publish articles opposing anti-Jewish measures. In the face of strong warnings by the government against pro-Jewish publications, Slachta continued to write and to teach adult classes on Christian social justice. She instructed members of the Society of Social Sisterhood to become familiar with her sympathy for the Jewish cause articulated in Lelek Szava, or The Voice of the Spirit. This familiarity prepared the sisters for future action.[10]

In the autumn of 1940, Slachta's mission drew her into direct contact with the Jews of Csíkszereda, whom the government had deported to Carpathia-Ruthenia. These people had already been forced to move twice before and they were absolutely destitute. Choices for escape were limited. Either they had to escape into the Russian woods and face viciously antisemitic Ukrainians, or remain in Ruthenia. The government made the first arrests in November, 1940, among Jews with leftist sympathies. Other charges, launched against Jews in the regions of Transylvania and Carpathia-Ruthenia, included ignoring vital national interests, spying, collaborating with the enemy, and encouraging dissent. The police launched trumped-up charges against the Jews if they could not find that Jews had broken the law.[11] Patriotic Hungarians living in these

---

10. Sister Natalie Palagyi, Sister of Social Service, *The Dove*, Los Angeles: Sisters of Social Service, 1946, 8. This pamphlet recounts their experiences of war.

11. This action was part of the eastward expulsion of Jews from Poland, Romania, Slovakia, Ruthenia, Transylvania, and the Sudetenland which uprooted age-old communities and disrupted the communities which received the refugees. See Martin Gilbert, *Atlas of the Holocaust*, New

areas were pleased with the removal of Jews from their region.

As members of the Sisters of Social Service, living in communities scattered throughout Hungary, reported on local situations, Slachta visited detention centers and transfer points and wrote summaries of her observations. She gathered information from police officials and priests at the local level where she acted as a power broker between the Jews and petty bureaucrats. She found that the deportation pattern was repeated again and again. Upon receiving an appeal from a family, Slachta contacted the local clergy and asked them to look into the circumstances. She offered money to officials and appealed to parish priests, bishops, and archbishops imploring them to use their influence with the government. She also tried to get high ranking government officials to halt deportations. While Hungary's regent, Nikolaus Horthy, attempted not to cave into the demands of popular antisemitism, his wife Ilona read about the horrid circumstances surrounding the deportations contained in Slachta's letters.[12] These detailed narratives reek of confused and deceitful policies orchestrated by both local and national authorities.

The following is a case in point. The Bernát Berkovits family contacted Slachta when the Hungarian Border Guard deported them to Ruthenia. After their transfer from one town to another, the city finance office ordered several Jewish families, including the Berkovits family, to pay be-

---

York: Macmillan, 1982; Majsai, 115-116. See also Bela Vago, "The Destruction of the Jews of Transylvania," *Hungarian-Jewish Studies*, ed. Randolph Braham, New York: World Federation of Hungarian Jewry, 1986, and Mária Schmidt, "Provincial Police Reports: New Insights into Hungarian Jewish History, 1941-1944," *Yad Vashem Studies, XIX*, ed. Aharon Weiss, Jerusalem: Yad Vashem, 1988, 233-268.

12. One of their members, Sara Schalkház worked for two years as a government social worker among Jewish families. See brochure "A Victim of Fraternal Charity;" SSSA.

tween twenty and one hundred Pengös (1 to 5 dollars) by noon on a given day. Slachta noted that the postman purposefully did not deliver the mail until after twelve o'clock. The following day, the police summoned 24 heads-of-households to pay the fees again. The Jews then had to leave without receipts because the local official announced that the proper administrator was not in his office. Again on November 7, the families received a summons regarding their legal status to appear at eight in the morning on November 8. The Jews were informed that they would be deported by one o'clock. The police refused to acknowledge their identity papers and passports. The families could take only as much as they could pack on their backs as they set out on the dogged existence as "stateless people."[13]

Tracing the victims' journey reveals the lack of a unified government policy. The families were forced into nearby forests where they were placed under armed guard. Those who could escape managed to do so. The armed guards abandoned the old, the sick, and the very young without shelter in rapidly deteriorating winter weather until November 14. Following a change in orders, authorities returned to take the deportees back. The survivors were in a weakened condition from cold and starvation. After an overnight rest they were transported back to their hometown. The Jewish victims were, just as in Germany after the Night of Broken Glass, forced to pay transportation

---

13. The value of the Hungarian Pengö equaled 0,26315789 grains of fine gold. The Pengö was adopted in 1925 to replace the Crown. During the 1941-42 period, the official value of the Pengö was approximately 20 cents. The black market price of the dollar, however ranged from 11 to 13 Pengös. Braham, *The Politics of Genocide*, 1994, n. 7, 71. For details on antisemitic legislature, see Yehuda Don. "Anti-Semitic Legislation in Hungary and their Implementation in Budapest – An Economic Analysis." ed. Randolph Braham. *The Tragedy of Hungarian Jewry. Essays, Documents, Depositions.* New York: Columbia University Press, 1986; Majsai, "The Deportation of Jews," 116-135.

costs. When they returned, the families faced deplorable living conditions. They slept on straw mats and existed without basic washing facilities. Men were forced to wash toilets; the guards addressed women with disrespect. Protests from the women spurred sentries to lock the women up separately from the men. Soon the government handed down another "corrected" order to the division captain, who again transported these families across border. This ordeal destroyed Jewish communities and uprooted and separated families. Law-abiding individuals became stateless nonentities.[14]

On December 9, 1940, Slachta wrote to the parish priest at Körösmező requesting assistance for the families who had suffered for over a month at the Hungarian-Romanian border. Helping the Jews was based, she said, on the Christian principle of brotherly love, an obligation to Christ, and patriotic devotion to Hungary. She urged the priest to go to the camp and ask why Jewish families had been interned. While there, she suggested that the priest might also investigate their living conditions and look into their return to their homes. She also offered him money to pay for the expenses of the families.[15]

Slachta's intervention was successful. The removal process stopped on the evening of December 9, when a telegram from the Ministry of Defense ordered the release of the detainees. It was the same day as the dateline on her letter to the parish priest. The report reveals that the captain in charge had received a telegram which ordered him immediately to release the Jews in his custody and to send them back home. Unfortunately, by this time six families were missing in the heavily forested border region. They either had fallen into the hands of the Russians or were

---

14. Summary report, December 1940, Majsai, 135-137.
15. Margit Slachta to parish priest at Körösmező, December 9, 1940, Majsai, 122-123.

frozen to death in a snowstorm. A halfhearted investigation concluded that no traces of lost families could be found. Other accounts showed that Jews had crossed the border at three places, were intercepted by a Russian patrol, put on three sleighs, and simply disappeared.[16]

Slachta regarded the forced border crossings as an abridgement of human rights. She noted that in the "selection process" (her words) the aged and disabled were among the first to go. She reported that a 79-year-old man, a seven-year-old boy, and two mentally disabled women were the first to be taken from their homes. Sister Sara Schalkház, a member of the Society, requested permission to cross the border and look for the missing but authorities refused, deflecting her to a larger maze of bureaucracy, the Foreign Ministry. In reality, the Ministry of Internal Affairs handled deportation matters. The government had obviously become aware of the humanitarian activities of Slachta and her sisters and was prepared to derail their efforts.[17]

Hungary – January 1941 – Slachta Appeals to Hungarian Officials

Shortly after Slachta's first attempt to help Jews, she came to the assistance of the family of Beno Schultz. Schultz believed that Slachta would understand the feelings of a mother who lost her children. She told Slachta, "My home is a house of tears." Hungarian officials, after deporting members of her family, claimed that they no longer fell under their jurisdiction. "The only thing that I cannot understand is why?" Schultz protested. "They themselves cannot tell us what our crime is, except that we are Jewish."

---

16. Majsai, 141-143 & 126-127; Sister of Social Service, Sara Schalkház in Tésco to Sister Petrá, at the motherhouse in Budapest, December 20, 1940.

17. Sister Schalkház in Tésco to Sister Petrá, December 20, 1940, Majsai, 126-127.

Slachta told Schultz that she would first confirm the details of abuses in writing and then she would write to the papal representative, Károly Pakocs. She counseled the distraught woman to put her trust in God.[18]

Slachta contacted the commissioner in charge of the internal affairs of the region. She told him that local "pashas" were uncooperative; they refused to establish the whereabouts of missing persons. The commissioner took over a month to respond to Slachta's demands and then denied any responsibility for the incidents. Slachta should see the Minister of the Interior or the Minister of Defense. On the commissioner's letter Slachta pencilled in, "This is the same old recipe; one body passing the buck to another."[19]

The deportation of the Schultz's alerted Slachta to the gravity of the situation. Quite independently of any pressure from Nazi Germany, Hungarian authorities had started the "resettlement" of non-Hungarian Jews. Between July and August, 1941, the government deported 20,000 Jews, not counting others who were displaced to the Ukraine.[20] Hearing of this, Slachta wrote to Ilona Horthy that she feared that things were happening in

> the name of Christianity which are contrary to its teachings. We raise our voices in opposition to the fact that officially-sanctioned mass atrocities can take place in our country. We do this as members of the human race, as Christians and as Hungarians. As members of the human race all our human feelings and natural instincts rebel against these acts. As Christians, we see these acts as direct contraventions of the commandments of God and our religion. As Hungarians, we are

---

18. Mrs. Beno Schultz to Margit Slachta, January 2, 1941, Majsai, 129-130; Margit Slachta to Mrs Beno Schultz, January 10, 1942, Majsai, 132.

19. Margit Slachta to Miklós Kozma, January 10, 1941, Majsai, 133-134; Miklós Kozma to Margit Slachta, February 18, 1941, Majsai, 143-145.

20. Majsai, 155.

unable to stand aside and watch the defilement of our Hungarian integrity embodied in these disgraceful acts.[21]

After this, Slachta joined a delegation to investigate the atrocity on the spot. Guards permitted only one person to visit the site, but that sufficed to confirm the Kamenets-Poldolsk massacre of "alien" Jews in August, 1941.[22] The event was a watershed for Slachta. In succeeding days her language became more shrill, her attitude toward higher authorities, more strident.

Slachta Protests Hungarian Antisemitism – 1942

By the middle of June, 1942, a second deportation from the city of Csíkszereda took place. Some time earlier, Jewish males were rounded up and interned in labor camps. Those left behind, the elderly, women and children struggled to survive on their own. When the boundaries of war between Nazi Germany and Russia shifted, local authorities made the preposterous charge that the presence of the families in the war zone threatened the security of the town and state, even though the fighting was still far away at this time. Police authorities first ordered the deportation of nineteen and then twenty-two families. This prompted the desperate Jewish women to write:

> We do not know why this took place but we can assume that someone aims to make the town free of Jews. We assume this because, since the unfortunate annexation of Transylvania, Jews have been almost constantly deported from our town.[23]

---

21. Slachta to Horthy, August 13, 1941, *Remembering for the Future*, Schmidt, 1988, 207.
22. Margit Slachta, "Speech delivered to the Hungarian Parliament," April 15, 1947, translated by Dr. Bela Piascek, SSSA.
23. Majsai, 113; Mrs. Karoly Herskovits to Margit Slachta, June 16, 1942, Majsai, 148.

The women knew that if the government transferred them, they would become part of the dispossessed, and be unable to provide for their children. One woman wrote that the most she could wish for was a delay of the transport ". . . until God returns our breadwinners to us."

The Csíkszereda women continued to see the whole situation as some huge mistake or bureaucratic foul up about which they could do nothing. They placed all their hopes in Slachta and believed that if she would intervene then the "misunderstanding" could be cleared up. Slachta knew better. She set out with newly drafted petitions, hoping to use her political influence to save the Csíkszereda Jews. Slachta and the sisters of the Service worked with a Jewish baroness, Edith Weiss, appealing to elite Hungarian women like Countess Móric Esterházy, to put a stop the atrocities.[24] For the most part this effort bore no fruit. Esterházy chose to help only in isolated instances, most probably, Jews with whom she had contacts before the imposition of anti-Jewish laws.[25]

Slachta did not work alone. The Society's houses served as an information net. In June 1942, Slachta received word from Sister Judit Veress about new deportations. Veress took the issue of deportation orders to Father Imre Sándor, who claimed that he could do nothing without knowing the details surrounding the situation. He referred both Slachta and Veress to the bishop. Slachta then contacted Archdeacon Ferenc Biró, a supporter of the Society and good friend of the police commissioner. Slachta believed that Biró could use his ecclesiastical authority to delay the transfer by contacting the police chief. Playing on Biró's sympathies, she asked rhetorically, to whom the

---

24. Braham, 1994, 86-92; 1151, n.45.
25. Margit Slachta to Countess Móric Esterházy, member of the Hungarian Red Cross, June 18, 1942, Majsai, 149-150; Margit Slachta to Baroness Edith Weiss, June 18, 1942, Majsai, 151.

Jews should turn for "merciful compassion" if not to the priests of the church and its loyal sons such as the police chief?[26] This worked; deportations were halted at least temporarily.

Unfortunately, Margit Slachta discovered that she could change Archdeacon Biró's mind but not his heart. Biró reluctantly conceded to help, but continued to believe that the government should move the Jews for the security of the country because they could not be trusted. He added that he was not the only one who thought it was for the best to move the Jews, and made it clear that he was unwilling to take on similar tasks again. Biró admonished Slachta not to ". . . involve me again because I do not accept this kind of church work."[27]

Slachta's activities established fundamental differences between her and the clergy. In 1942, the Hungarian parliament authorized the final phase of the expropriation of Jewish property. Justinian Cardinal Seredi, the Prince Primate of Hungary, justified the legislation as being God's will. He argued that ". . . we are to ascribe to the will of God . . . the laws of the state as well." Slachta challenged this conflated argument which equated state principles with those of the church. Although the Hungarian clergy rejected her activism, Slachta sought support outside Hungary from German and Dutch bishops who also found themselves in conflict with Nazi antisemitism. The sisters reproduced sermons of these foreign bishops, along with

---

26. Margit Slachta to Archdeacon Ferenc Biró, June 22, 1942, Majsai, 153-154.
27. Sister Judit Veress witnessed atrocities in 1941. She wrote "My heart was aching when I read of these actions which shame Christianity. I was myself witness to similar scenes while I was there last year." Sándor then sent Sister Judit to Count Gusztáv Majlath, Bishop of Gyulafehervar who was sympathetic to the plight of Jewish families. Sister Judit Veress to Margit Slachta, Kolozsvár, June 22, 1942, Majsai, 151-152. Letter from Archdeacon Ferenc Biró to Margit Slachta, dated July 17, 1941, but cited as July 17, 1942. Majsai, 163.

correspondence between them and Slachta, and sent copies to members of the Hungarian hierarchy.[28] At the same time, the Society pressed for social justice based on Christian principles. Through their newspaper, The Voice of the Spirit, they carried their message to thousands of workers, particularly women, informing them of ways in which they could help Jews. As antisemitism increased in Hungary, the Society worked harder to teach ordinary people the principles of Christian social justice. Society members traveled to more than fifty towns to show films and give lectures against war and racism. In some places as many as three to four thousand people attended. Slachta taught that racism sowed seeds of division. People should follow, instead, the Christian ideal of universal love that would stand in opposition to violent attacks against their Jewish neighbors.[29]

Slovakia 1942-43: Slachta Appeals to Pius XII

In spite of its harsh anti-Jewish measures, Hungary became a haven for foreign Jews until 1944. Distressing reports, arriving from Slovakia, motivated Slachta to get caught up in rescuing Slovakian Jews. Catholic Slovakia was essentially a German satellite state. Although its president, Josef Tiso, was a priest, Slovakia aped German antisemitism. The government expropriated Jewish owned businesses and set down restrictions which expelled people from their professions by spring, 1940. As Jewish economic security deteriorated, leaving many homeless, the government drove Jews into forced labor camps. On September 10, 1941, the Codex Judaicum, based on the Nuremberg Laws, removed all legal rights of Jews. Large scale deportation "transports"

---

28. After the war, Slachta expressed a different view of Cardinal Seredi in her speech to Parliament. "Speech delivered to the Hungarian Parliament," April 15, 1947, SSSA.

29. Palagyi, *The Dove*, 8-9.

began in early 1942. Before summer's end Slovakia had deported 60,000 people or 60 percent of the Slovak Jewish population. Slachta feared that Slovakia's genocide would spread to Hungary.

In April, 1942, Slachta appealed to the Hungarian hierarchy to intervene. Inundating the Hungarian bishops with petitions, Slachta tried to persuade them to contact Slovakian church leaders to condemn the deportations. At Easter time, Slachta witnessed Jewish persecution in Bratislava. She saw the pain in the faces of the young men who were forced into work camps, and the young women who were sent off to work on the eastern front. Even more disconcerting was the fact that Slovakia paid Germany 500 Marks (about 125 dollars) for every Jew that the Germans transported out of the country. Passing on these details, Slachta assured the bishops that her information was from "extremely reliable sources," but they were unresponsive.[30] Slachta pointed out the hypocrisy of the Catholic church in Slovakia, arguing that while it denied Jews their legal rights, Christians were unaffected. Catholics continued to attend church but refused to provide shelter for their beleaguered neighbors.[31]

Hoping that her friend, Bishop Gyula Zichy of Kalosca, would help her, Slachta shared her belief with him that Christian morality called for political action based on higher standards than those required by the state. She opposed state policies that clashed with Christian principles. She wrote, "My conscience tells me that I am an accomplice if I have not tried to do everything in my power to put an end to these acts." Slachta appealed for the same commitment to Christianity from the Hungarian bishops

30. Margit Slachta letter to Bishop of Kalocsa, April 27, 1942, Schmidt, 1988, 208; Majsai, 117, 150.

31. Margit Slachta letter to Bishop of Kalocsa, April 27, 1942, Schmidt, 1988, 208.

and urged them to act "against this Satanism." She anticipated that the bishops would defer to the Hungarian government on the premise of noninvolvement in the affairs
of another country. To this, Slachta argued, "Surely there
are no political frontiers before God." Slachta prodded the
Hungarian bishops to contact their Slovakian counterparts
and even asked the Vatican to excommunicate Tiso and his
accomplices. She believed that if the church ignored this
problem, it's moral standing throughout the world would
be damaged or lost.[32]

Several days after the Slovakian deportations had begun, Slachta implored the Bishop of Csanád, Gyula
Glattfelder, to risk action.

> I think that if there is no way to take risks, any cause
> will fail and the cause of the church, its possessions
> and schools will be lost . . . I think that if the bishops
> are prepared to take steps, they should take action
> against the [Slovak] Prime Minister and practically
> force the Minister of Interior to halt the poisoning of
> people's minds by hatred.[33]

Unfortunately, Bishop Glattfelder argued that he did not
have the "authorization" to act unilaterally. Bishops could
not speak frankly, he asserted, because they feared "unimaginable reprisals." He felt that saving Christians of
Jewish ancestry was more important. Glattfelder stated that
the atrocities in Slovakia were only alleged, and advised
Slachta not to get involved. But Slachta knew that "deportation meant death."

Meeting a dead end with the bishops, Slachta decided
to turn to the pope himself. Slachta's timing was faultless.
Just when it appeared likely that the remaining 25,000 Jews,

---

32. Margit Slachta letter to Bishop of Kalocsa, April 27, 1942, Schmidt, 1988,
    208.
33. Margit Slachta to Bishop of Csanád, Gyula Glattfelder, April 29, 1942,
    Schmidt, 1988, 209.

those who had converted to Christianity, were going to be "transported," she met with the pope on March 13, 1943. An audience was arranged for her through an old acquaintance from the United States, Francis Cardinal Spellman, Archbishop of New York.

Slachta recorded her meeting with Pius XII in her diary. She said that her hands were clammy when usually they were dry and "tears were welling up in my eyes." She attributed her state of mind to the gravity of her message and that she would be bringing him woeful and anguishing news. When the pope came into the room, he asked her to be seated, while he remained standing. Slachta told him that she represented more than 20,000 Slovakian deportees who were facing untimely deaths. Slachta offered many details, and showed him documents which the Hungarian Jewish Welfare Bureau and the Jewish community of Pest had given to her. Then she suggested that if the Vatican could provide food and housing during the impending internment that the Slovakian government might possibly postpone the deportation. This would counter the excuse of Slovak authorities that unemployed and homeless Jews were a burden the government could not handle. Slachta wrote:

> . . . . He listened to me all the way through. . . . He expressed his shock. . . . I can say the following: he listened to me but said very little. I will never forget the way he looked at me. It was deep, deadly serious and beneficent. I felt deeply moved that evening and even the next day.[34]

Actually, Pius could not have been suprised by Slachta's news. The pope had learned about the deportations and mass killings through reports from the Archbishop of Vienna, Theodor Cardinal Innitzer. Papal nuncio Giuseppe

---

34. Slachta's own essay, typed original, 13th March 1943 in the possession of Ilona Mona, Schmidt, 1988, 209.

Burzio had kept the Vatican informed about the events taking place in Slovakia, and the nuncio in Budapest, Angelo Rotta, had already urged the pope to use his influence with Tiso to stop the deportations.[35] At any rate, the pope told Slachta that she could have a clear conscience in the matter, and that

> The Holy See has done and is doing all which is in its power on behalf of the Jews, in all the areas where they are the object of odious measures; and particularly, in regard to the case at hand, on behalf of the Slovak Jews.[36]

This was a stock phrase used repeatedly by the Vatican during the Holocaust years.

If Pope Pius's response disappointed Slachta, she did not record this in her diary. While in Rome, she met Cardinal Spellman and outlined a plan for the United States to halt the deportations. This proposal was a further elaboration of her initial overture to the Vatican, and comprised the following "if-then" sequences. If Slovakia should plan to carry out the deportations, then the United States would offer refuge. If Slovakia gave up its deportation plan, then the United States could intervene on behalf of mistreated German soldiers who were Russian prisoners of war. If the Slovakian government should permit the Jews to remain, but required a sum, say of 150,000 Swiss Francs monthly, then the United States would offer to pay the amount to Slovakia in dollars. If the United States could agree to these conditions, then Spain, who had a diplomat in Slovakia, could offer to be the guarantor of Jewish interests in Slovakia. If Spain would permit transfer passes to Jews, then the United States could declare its willingness to grant permanent refugee status after the war. Slachta begged

---

35. John Morley, *Vatican Diplomacy and the Jews During the Holocaust: 1939-1943*, New York: Ktav Publishing, 1980, 80-81; Braham, 1994, 1212.

36. Morley, 91.

Spellman to "remember [the Jews] in their extreme suffering." Slachta's plan for the rescue of Slovakian Jews met a dead end in the United States Department of State.[37]

Slachta's audience with the pope may have helped stave off the 1943 deportations and further executions in Slovakia. After horrific reports arrived at the Vatican about Auschwitz, the Slovakian bishops finally censored the Tiso government. In an about face from the previous year, church officials set out to protect Jews, particularly Catholic converts.[38] But Pope Pius never publicly condemned the atrocities in Slovakia.

The Jews left behind in Slovakia rose up at the end of September, 1944, but met defeat. The remaining 12 – 13,000 were transported to Auschwitz, Sachsenhausen, and Theresienstadt. The final figures for the Catholic state of Slovakia range around a total of 70,000 Jewish men, women, and children, who were deported to Poland in sixty-eight transports and murdered. Less than 4,000 Jews survived.[39] When the time arrived for the final push by the Nazis to deport the remaining Jews from Slovakia in 1944, rescue work in Budapest engrossed Margit Slachta.

---

37. Margit Slachta to Francis Cardinal Spellman, spring 1943, Schmidt, 1987, 59.

38. Mária Schmidt, "Destruction of Slovakian Jews as Reflected in Hungarian Police Reports" ed. Randolph Braham, *Studies on the Holocaust in Hungary*, New York: Columbia University Press, 1990, 27.

39. Pius XII remains a subject of great historiographical importance regarding issues surrounding church responsibility for moral, spiritual, and practical leadership. For a thorough and current discussion regarding these issues, see John T. Pawlikowski, "The Vatican and the Holocaust: Unresolved Issues," *Jewish-Christian Encounters over the Centuries: Symbiosis, Prejudice, Holocaust, Dialogue*, eds. Marvin Perry and Frederick M. Schweitzer, New York: Peter Lang, 1994; Braham, 1994, 1214-1215; Others hold that the Vatican did not in any way warn the Slovakian government that what they were doing was in direct opposition with the teachings of the Catholic church. Ladislav Lipscher, "The Jews of Slovakia, 1939-1945" *The Jews of Czechoslovakia*, ed. Avigdor Dagan, Philadelphia: Jewish Publication Society of America, 1984, 312-313, 242.

Slachta Feeds Budapest Jews – 1944

As war drew closer to the Balkan peninsula and the consequences of deportation became clearer to the Hungarian
Jewish community, Budapest became a magnet for any Jew
who could manage to get there. Aware of their predicament, Slachta sought to alert Christians to their broader
responsibilities toward all people. "With what measure ye
mete, it shall be measured to you again." She urged Hungarian women to reach out to the Jewish refugees, particularly the men who were in forced labor camps. She called
on them to accept Jewish refugees. "Dare to rid your heart
of ignorance, disdain, and hatred in this deadly serious
age, dare to accept deep in your heart another mother and
her son as your fellow human beings, dare to bear her pain
and help her to carry her cross." Slachta called on women
to influence the men in their families who were in the
military or had charge of the forced labor camps to treat
inmates with compassion. She reminded Hungarian
women that they would hope for the same if their relatives
were facing a similar fate.

For her outspoken pro-Jewish stance, the Hungarian
government condemned Slachta as "unpatriotic" and
branded her as a traitor. Undeterred, Slachta stiffened her
position. "I stand, without compromise, on the foundation
of Christian values; that is, I profess that love obliges us to
accept natural laws for our fellow-men without exception,
which God gave and which cannot be taken away." Following such forthrightness, authorities tried to suppress
Slachta's community newspaper and finally succeeded in
the spring of 1944.[40]

In 1941, the estimated Jewish population of Budapest
was about 250,000; by 1944 it had grown to 280,000. When
the Nazis marched into the city on 19 March, 1944, most

---

40. Palagyi, *The Dove*, 9, SSSA; Majsai, 118-119.

Hungarians breathed more freely. At least, they were not Russian troops. But for Jews an identification and isolation process began. Jews were ordered to wear a sign of their racial origins, the six-inch yellow Star of David. These laws offended Slachta immensely. Then the Hungarian government acceded to Nazi demands and began deporting Jews. On April 16, 1944, 92 trains left Hungary for Auschwitz. By early July, the countryside had been cleared of Jews and deportation transports began departing from Budapest. In the weeks that followed the fascist Arrow Cross government collaborated with the Nazis, expelling 437,000 Jews to Auschwitz.[41]

During this frightful period Slachta provided shelter for Jews at the motherhouse in Budapest and elsewhere across Hungary. During the 1944 Easter season, Slachta called all members of the Society to a retreat in Budapest. In the silence of the retreat, Sister Margit asked the following questions:

> Is it the conviction of every Sister of Social Service that a moral organization can be safe for the future only when it lives up to its moral convictions? . . . Are we willing in the name of fraternal love to take the risk of being interned, or carried away, of the Community being dissolved, or even of losing our own lives? If so, even if all these things were to happen, yet if in the soul of every Sister of Social Service, the ideals of Christianity still live, then the Community will be found worthy to have a future and will deserve life even if only one Sister of Social Service were left alive. . . . On the other hand, what does it help us if our work, our property, our lives are left to us but when we come to give account we have to hide our face shamefully before the eyes of God.[42]

---

41. Moshe Y. Herczl, *Christianity and the Holocaust of Hungarian Jewry*, trans. Joel Lerner, New York: New York University Press, 1993, 174, 180; Braham, "Data Related to the Ghettoization and Deportation of Hungarian Jewry by Operational Zones and Gendarmerie Districts," 1994, 674, 859.

Slachta was willing to risk everything for which she and the Society had worked. They did this in the name of Christianity. After the retreat she inspired members to return to their houses, which stretched from the borders of Romania to Germany, and harbor refugees until the end of the war. The sisters hid Jews behind walls and in cellars. They allowed families to come out only in the safety of the night. Rescue activities raised suspicions about the community houses, which became the object of constant raids. The sisters housed more than a thousand Jews during the Nazi siege.[43]

For a short period it was still possible for Jews to avoid deportation by converting. Members of the Society taught religion courses day and night instructing Jews in the fundamentals of Catholicism, preparing them for baptism, although both the sisters and the Jews knew this was just a subterfuge.[44] In October, 1944, after the Arrow Cross had taken control of the Hungarian government, the newly baptized were no longer protected. Decrees forced all Jews to move into specially designated apartment buildings in ghettos that were off limits to visitors. This did not deter Slachta and her community. They simply changed from their grey habits to street clothing. Some sisters even wore a Star of David so that they could move into the ghetto more freely. The Society supplied and distributed food, clothing, and medicine to the now isolated families. As Nazi control tightened, the sisters worked with the Red

42. Palagyi, *The Dove*, 10, SSSA.

43. Palagyi, *The Dove*, 10, SSSA.

44. Palagyi, *The Dove*, 11; Slachta, "Speech delivered to the Hungarian Parliament" SSSA; Jenö Levai, *Hungarian Jewry and the Papacy: Pope Pius XII did not remain silent*. trans. J. R. Foster, London: Sands & Co., 1967, 23; Haim Genizi and Naomi Blank, "The Rescue Efforts of Bnei Akiva in Hungary During the Holocaust," ed. Aharon Weis, *Yad Vashem Studies, XXIII*, Jerusalem: Yad Vashem, 1993, 192-193; see also, Gabor Sztehlo, *In the Hands of God*, translator, Judit Zinner, (Budapest, 1994).

Cross cooking for more than 2,000 people and distributing medicines supplied by the papal nunciature.[45]

In early July, 1944, the transport trains started to roll out of Budapest. Slachta, with the aid of Catholic lay women, set up food and drink stands along the route for the deportees. Recognizing that these actions would endanger the safety of Society members, Slachta advised those who were afraid to seek safety outside the city, but she remained in Budapest to do what could be done for the Jews. The government had long ago branded Slachta's activities as unpatriotic. Members of the Arrow Cross, Hungary's version of the Nazi party, beat Slachta in the autumn of 1944, but spared her life. Another member of the Society was less fortunate; Sister Sara Schalkház was executed along with six Jewish refugees in December, 1944. Slachta recognized that a similar fate awaited her. When the Arrow Cross came to the motherhouse with a warrant for her arrest, Slachta deceived them by answering that she could not read the name on the warrant. The Arrow Cross returned for her again, but by early January, 1945, Slachta had gone into hiding in a nearby Carmelite convent. She remained there until the Soviet army liberated Hungary at the end of February, 1945.[46]

Conclusion

Margit Slachta's Christian response to the plight of the Jewish people points out a significant conflict of faith. She confronted the church hierarchy by expressing her belief in a Catholic theology which proclaims God's love for all humanity. In fact, her beliefs and activities challenged the state and the entrenched church hierarchy. Her publica-

45. Palagyi, *The Dove*, 11; Slachta, "Speech to Hungarian Parliament," SSSA; See Herczl regarding the condition in the Budapest ghettoes, 218.

46. Natalie Palagyi interview with author, Buffalo, NY – Milwaukee, WI, March 19, 1994; Palagyi, *The Dove*, 11-13, SSSA; Schmidt, 1988, 210.

tions and open letters confronted ecclesiastical and provincial officials by advocating fellowship and unity over nation and race.

Slachta's activities on behalf of the Jewish mothers of Csíkszereda demonstrates the power of one voice raised in protest. She did not wait until the end of the war to censure the insane antisemitic policies of Hungary, Slovakia, and Nazi Germany but responded at the outset, when she first lent a hand to the desperate women of Csíkszereda. Her reliance on an extensive circle of support, which gained her an audience with the pope, probably contributed to the delay of the second phase of deportations from Slovakia. Her leadership in Budapest gave Catholic lay women the courage to risk their own lives in the face of German and Hungarian fascists.

After the war, the Hungarians reelected Slachta to parliament. When Hungary fell under the influence of Stalin's eastern block, Slachta's principles would not allow her to agree with the atheism of the new government. Fearing for her life, Slachta abandoned her parliamentary seat. At the urging of the Sisters of Social Service, she agreed to leave Hungary. Slachta escaped to the border, hidden in a hay wagon, where she crawled under the barbed wire fence separating East and West.[47] Slachta is credited with saving 2,000 or more Jews.[48] Yad Vashem, the Holocaust Martyrs' and Heroes' Remembrance Authority has honored Slachta as a Righteous Gentile.[49]

---

47. Sister Natalie Palagyi letter to author, January 5, 1994.
48. Majsai, 118.
49. G. Rocca, Dizionario degli instituti de perfezione, vol. 8, col. 1435; Uri Asaf. "Christian Support for Jews during the Holocaust in Hungary" ed. Randolph Braham, New York: Columbia University Press, 1990, 71, 97, 99; Braham, 1994, 1199.

Chapter Four

I Will Not Be a Bystander!

Germaine Ribière

Entries from a Journal

We shall begin this chapter with an unpublished document, a wartime diary in the form of a simple black notebook. Its author is Germaine Ribière, who was then a university student in Paris. At the time of the first entry she was twenty-two years old.[1]

May 14, 1941. This morning they began rounding up Jews, 7,000 of them in the fourth *arondissement.* Most of them are said to be Polish Jews, and the poorest ones at that. Has the great dance begun in France? My God, give me strength.

They had to be ready in an hour and were told to take along food for one day. We don't know where they are going . . . I ache for them in my whole being, I ache for my Jewish brothers and sisters . . . My God, permit me to suffer with them. Accept their suffering, make it life-giving.

May 27, 1941. For the past two weeks the sky has become more and more overcast. The church, the hierarchy, remain silent. They allow the truth to be profaned. Father Lallier told me that there are more urgent things for us to worry about than the Jews. Last Saturday, when we told him that

---

1. Parts of this journal appear in my paper given at Oxford, "Can the Few Become the Many?," and published in *Remembering for the Future*, Vol. I, pp. 235-237. Oxford and New York: Pergamon Press, 1989.

we wanted to write something about the church and the temporal order, he urged us not to speak about racism . . .

The tide is rising, rising. I am afraid that one of these days, when we wake up, it will be too late and we shall all have become Nazis. I am afraid, because people are asleep. Those who should keep watch are the ones who put others to sleep. We must shout the truth no matter what the cost. But who will do it? I know that there are Christians who are willing to accept martyrdom if need be, but they do not know what is happening. They wait for a voice, and the voice does not speak. We must pray that it will speak.

June 14, 1941. France has betrayed her soul, and Nazism is gaining the upper hand. All genuine values are dragged in the dust. We no longer have any honor. Pétain has become the French Hitler. The great dance has begun and the world is blind. It is blind because it is afraid of death. The clergy remain passive. As in Austria, they accept what is happening.

I am in Paris for a few days, we have to put the affairs [of the J.E.C. – the Catholic Student Movement] in order. I have the impression that the earth is shaking, and I am shaking along with it . . . Often I long to go away, all alone. But this would be running away. The world is our stage leading to God. We must not burn this stage, we must live it to the best of our ability.

August 31, 1941. Catholic Action is in total confusion. There is chaos everywhere, an immense confusion . . . And in the midst of it all a small number of people who see clearly . . . But those who, with all their might, fight against a policy of collaboration with Germany because they know what is at stake, they are accused of mixing religion and politics, the throne and the altar!This week I visited two camps.[2] Total contempt for the human being. At Cervières-le-Château the guard, a little drunk, grabbed a young Jewish boy by the throat, held him motionless for a few moments, then had his fun brushing his face with the toilet broom – and it was not clean. Many other similar scenes.

Yesterday I visited Rabbi Deutsch [of Limoges, her hometown]. I told him to make use of me in any way he can. I am willing to do anything for them, with the help of God. I cannot run away.

April 14, 1942. Since my last entry this immense history of the Jewish people continues. Man sinks each day more deeply into the mire of sin. The camps continue to run, the world of Satan heaves beneath our feet. But Christ will conquer in the end . . .

June 1, 1942. For the past month much tension: visits to the internment camps, absence there of any Catholic witness. Always the problem of the human being torn by sin. . . .

June 11, 1942. The problem of the Jews – no, the mystery of the Jews. The mystery of the human being. I try to confront all this. Always alone, in solitude, alone with Christ.

November 14, 1942. The Germans crossed the demarcation line on November 11, armistice day [of the first World War]. I am crushed by the misery all around me.

February 4, 1943. Every day the evil grows. Nazism tightens its grip, Catholics are asleep. Last Wednesday, January 27, the whole team of *Amitié Chrétienne* was arrested by the Gestapo [cf. also pp. below]. Thursday evening I went to the archdiocese [of Lyon] to ask what could be done about the children and the *Amitié*. The Cardinal's [Gerlier] private

---

2. Internment camps in the south of France had been established in the 1930s for refugees from the Spanish civil war. Under Vichy they were used for Jews, as well as non-Jews, who were interned under inhuman conditions in camps such as Gurs, Rivesâltes, Récébédou etc.

secretary told me, 'The Cardinal has enough such stories, he certainly won't go along.' Later I called the Cardinal. He referred me to G, dean of the law faculty at Lyon . . . All of them, one after the other, are cracking under the strain. I don't understand. We are told to bear witness to Christ! I am tired of this ridiculous prudence, of this fear of physical death!

June 16, 1943. I was speaking with Chanoine T. [professor of the Catholic faculty of Lille, one of its famous 'pontifs' – the word is hers], about Christian ethics. 'We must not try to put Christian ethics into everything!' This remark was followed by an explanation of St. Thomas. . . . Strange: under the guise of St. Thomas they try to slip in Maurras![3]

Why do they talk of Christian morality as if it were a spice which one may or may not add to life, to every action, every moment? Why this refusal to see Christ everywhere, as if all that is good, and upright, and true in the law did not belong to him? It is as if we were ashamed of him. We no longer profess him in public because, in our hearts, we don't give him all that is his, we don't recognize all that comes from him. We speak of discretion instead of cowardice, and under the pretext of being discreet we betray, scandalize and, through a clever juggling act, keep our consciences clean. . . .

In reading these texts one is led to ask: Who was this young woman who identified so passionately with the plight of

---

3. Charles Maurras was the leader of the *Action Française*, an influencial, conservative, nationalistic movement. It enjoyed great prestige after World War I among French Catholics of the Right, to many of whom it appeared as the guarantor of patriotism and family values, a bulwark against democracy and liberalism. Its journal, by the same name, was the chief organ of an integrist, anti-modernist, antisemitic Catholicism. Condemned by Rome in 1926 the *Action Française* nevertheless retained a strong hold on many Catholics, and left its imprint on the antisemitism of the Vichy government.

the Jews, who saw so clearly and agonized over the failure of her church, and who was determined, come what may, not to be a bystander? What enabled her to become a tireless worker for the rescue of Jews, a clear-sighted, committed member of the Resistance, trusted collaborator of Fathers P. Chaillet, A. Glasberg, and Roger Braun, and member of the core team of *Amitié Chrétienne*? Time and again I asked myself these questions, asked them of those who knew her.

From my work in the Yad Vashem archives of the Department of the Righteous I knew that Germaine had been honored by Yad Vashem on March 19, 1968. Her file (No. 367) contains a letter from Louis Domb to Israeli ambassador Walter Eytan dated July 19, 1966:

> . . . If the two sons of my wife are alive today, it is thanks to the actions of Germaine Ribière, not counting the help she has given me personally and which I have thus far not mentioned. When the Germans occupied the south and arrived in Limoges on November 12, 1942 they came to arrest me soon after, because I was on their black list due to my Resistance activities while in Paris. Germaine Ribière hid me, first for some days in Limoges; then, during several weeks, with a country pastor of the region. After that I joined the Resistance of Corrèze. . . .

The file told me little else. In those relatively early days "decisions were sometimes made based on personal knowledge of the case, rather than on documentary data."[4]

As I began my research in France her name kept coming up. "Have you seen Germaine Ribière yet?" interviewees would ask me. "She was at the heart of things, her testimony is crucial." It was not difficult to meet her. She suggested over the phone that we meet at the noon Mass at Notre Dame des Champs and then have lunch together. I readily agreed.

---

4. Letter from Mordecai Paldiel to the author, November 24, 1993.

On the way to the restaurant a small incident took place which told me much about this woman whom I had only just met. We were engrossed in conversation when she suddenly interrupted herself. "I am worried about this little girl, I wonder if she has lost her mother." I had noticed, vaguely, a little girl in front of us on the sidewalk, about two years old, alone, but I had not really "seen" her. Germaine had seen, and worried. As it turned out the mother was close by, walking ahead of the child. As I came to know Germaine in the months that followed and to learn of the extraordinary things she had done during the war I realized how much of a piece she is. She is Germaine Ribière because she notices a little girl who may be lost and in need of help in the middle of Paris in 1985, just as the Jews needed help during the war.

Let us now return to the journal entries with which this chapter opened. We shall use them as a lense through which to gain a better understanding of the situation and attitude of the official Roman Catholic Church of France at that time and, against this background, of Germaine herself. What caused her despondency and deep disappointment over the church of which she was a faithful member? How was she able to remain within this church, despite her discouragement, while sustaining her determination "not to be a bystander"?

Pétain and the Catholic Church[5]

The rapidity of France's defeat in May-June 1940 left the country shattered both physically and morally. So great

5. See the following works on this subject: Xavier de Montclos *et al.*, eds. *Englises et Chrétiens dans la IIe Guerre Mondiale. La région Rhone-Alpes.* Lyon: Presses Universitaires, 1978. Centre de Documentation Juive Contemporaine, *La France et la Question Juive.* 1940/1944. Paris: Sylvie Messinger, 1981. Jacques Duquesne, *Les Catholiques Français sous l'Occupation.* Paris: Grasset, 1966; rev. ed. 1986. Michael R. Marrus and Robert O. Paxton, *Vichy France and the Jews.* New York: Schocken Books, 1983. Pierre Pierrard, *Juifs et Catholiques Français.* Paris: Fayard, 1970.

were the trauma and sense of humiliation that the armistice, signed in the begining of June, was greeted by the majority of people with a mixture of relief and gratitude: three weeks of horror and nightmare, of roads clogged with refugees, were at an end.

The relief was all the more palpable because the man who signed the armistice and who headed the new government of Vichy was a man of almost legendary stature: the victor of Verdun, Marshal Philippe Pétain. To quote only one voice, that of Cardinal Suhard of Paris, in a speech given two days after the armistice: "Is not Marshal Pétain the Frenchman without reproach, the Frenchman who desires only to serve?. . . . When, in a difficult and dark hour, such a head of state speaks, we owe him our trust!"

The support given to Pétain initially by the country at large was particularly strong among Catholics, who had not fared well under the Third Republic and the government of Léon Blum. Pétain recognized and skillfully exploited the sense of discrimination from which the church suffered. He restored privileges that had been revoked, and began using a vocabulary in his speeches with which Catholics felt at home, though he had never been a particularly "good" Catholic himself. He spoke of "our sins" that had caused the defeat, which could thus be interpreted as God's just punishment on a France that had been unfaithful to her Christian vocation as "oldest daughter of the church." He spoke of the need for repentance, for moral and spiritual regeneration, terms familiar and dear to Catholics. Pétain thus won, at least for a time, the loyalty even of those church leaders who, in the summer of 1942, were to protest publicly the inhumanity of Vichy's anti-Jewish measures. This also explains the famous words of Cardinal Gerlier when he welcomed Pétain to Lyon in October 1940: "Pétain is France, France is Pétain." The first months of the Vichy regime have been aptly characterized as "a time of trust and illusion."[6] It was precisely in those early months that the anti-Jewish legislation began to be put in place, a legislation which pushed Jews more and more to the margins of French society in the months that followed.

The summer of 1942 was a turning point, both in the persecution of Jews and in the public's response to it. As the deportations gained momentum and the trains rolled throughout France toward the East, many who until then had been silent began to speak out. This was true also of the Catholic hierarchy: for a brief period it assumed a role of moral leadership. In less than one month five bishops issued official protests, two of them in a prophetic voice. The archbishop (later Cardinal) of Toulouse, Jules-Gérard Saliége, was the first to speak. On August 23, 1942 he ordered a letter to be read in the churches of his diocese in which he passionately decried the inhuman treatment of Jews;

> .... That children, women, men, fathers and mothers, should be treated like a vile herd of cattle, the members of the same family separated from each other and sent to an unknown destination – it was reserved for our times to witness this tragic spectacle. Why does the right to asylum no longer exist in our church? ....[7]

Inspired by Saliège's example the bishop of the neighboring diocese of Montauban, Pierre-Marie Théas, in turn wrote a pastoral letter, no less passionate in tone, which was read the following Sunday, August 30:

> I must make heard the indignant protest of the Christian conscience, and I proclaim that all men, Aryan or non-Aryan, are brothers, because they are created by

---

6. Renée Bédarida, *Témoignage Chrétien. Les Armes de l'Esprit* (1941-1944). Paris: Les Editions Ouvrières, 1977.

7. This document is found in all histories dealing with the subject of the French church under the Nazis, e.g., Marrus and Paxton, n. 5 above.

the same God; that all, whatever their race or religion, are entitled to respect from individuals and the state. The current antisemitic measures are in contempt of human dignity, a violation of the most sacred rights of the individual and of the family . . ..[8]

Three more declarations followed in September: from Cardinal Gerlier of Lyon, Bishop Delay of Marseille, and Bishop Mousseron of Albi. While deploring the inhumane treatment of Jews, both Gerlier and Delay mentioned "the problem" posed for France by the refugees and asserted the government's right to "take all appropriate steps."

Even though these last declarations excused the Vichy government, their impact on French public opinion was considerable. Perhaps this impact can best be gauged by Vichy's attempt to have Saliège's letter suppressed (without success). Police reports dealing with the Jewish question that were kept throughout France between the summer of 1942 and the fall of the Vichy regime in 1944 also express frequent concern about the influence of the bishops' declarations on the rank and file of French Catholics. "What a tragedy that this (protest) happened only in the fall of 1942. If all this had been said in 1941, when the deportations had as yet hardly begun!" writes the historian Georges Wellers.[9]

Only against this background can the frustration and pain expressed in Germaine Ribière's journal be understood. We shall now supplement the journal entries from other sources.

The date of the first entry quoted above, May 1941, is significant. It antedates by more than a year the first official Catholic protests against the persecution of the Jews. *Témoignage Chrétien*, which was to become one of the main

---

8. *ibid.*
9. Georges Wellers, quoted in my Oxford paper, n. 1 above, p.235.

organs of Christian spiritual resistance, had not yet been founded. The first issue appeared six months later, in November 1941.[10] Thus Germaine Ribiére was without any support from the official church. She speaks of her vain hope for a prophetic voice, a voice that could galvanize Catholics who might be willing to give their lives, if only they knew what was happening and had some guidance. "But the voice does not speak. We must pray that it will speak. . . . The church, the hierarchy, remain silent. They allow the truth to be profaned" (5/27/41).

Two weeks earlier, on May 14, the Germans had begun to round up Jews in Paris, starting with *Le Marais*, the city's ancient, and still present-day, Jewish quarter. The first entry quoted dates from that day. Germaine agonizes over the terrible scenes that are taking place in the *Marais* – one has the impression that she was an eye witness to them, Many years later she recalled this event and added more details.[11]

She was living in a residence for university students in Paris at that time. A fellow student, Marie Hervé, whose mother was director of a school in the rue des Archives in the *Marais*, came to her room shortly after 1 p.m. Marie was distraught as she described what was happening. "'My mother did all she could to save the children, but it was no use. We are desperate, something must be done!' I told Marie, 'as Christians we can't just stand here with our hands in our pockets. We must do something, we must make people aware of what is going on.' But what to do? We could not go down into the streets because we didn't

---

10. *Les Cahiers du Témoignage Chrétien* became one of the chief tools of Christian spiritual resistance. Founded in Lyon by the Jesuits of Fourvière the periodical was published claudestinely between November 1941 and July 1944, and distributed throughout France. The April-May, 1942 issue was devoted entirely to antisemitism. See Bédarida, n. 6 above.

11. Ribière in de Montclos *et al., op. cit.*, p. 205. All translations of this and other French texts are by the author.

want to be arrested needlessly. We had to continue our work."

Germaine was a member of the J.E.C. (Christian Student Movement), in charge at that time of its young women's division. She decided to call a joint meeting of the young men and women students at the church of Saint-Etienne-du-Mont near the Sorbonne, and to organize a prayer vigil there as a way of saying, We protest what has happened. "We met with our chaplain, Father Lallier, who was also the secretary of the archdiocese (and who later became a bishop). . . . I asked one of my friends to speak at the meeting of the children's arrest and of our projected vigil, so that he would lend his support to our project. At one point Father Lallier turned to me and said, 'I admire your charity, Mademoiselle, it is truly admirable. Yes, there is the Jewish problem; there is also the problem of Alsace. But please, understand, we too have our problem – our schools' (subsidies for parochial schools had just recently begun to be granted by the government). "I left the meeting and told my friends: 'If, in order to be a Christian, I must leave Catholic Action, I leave this evening!' This was the sort of climate in which we had to work."[12]

Catholic Action was obviously in as great a state of disarray as the rest of the French church, unclear as to where its duty lay. "There is chaos everywhere, an immense confusion . . . In the midst of it all a few people who see clearly . . . Those who fight against a policy of collaboration . . . are accused of mixing religion and politics, the throne and the altar" (August 31).

The above entries were written while Germain was in Paris. She returned there several times for Resistance activities even after she had moved to Lyon. But the situation in the south was no better.[13] She tells of one instance when,

---

12. *ibid.*, p. 206.

upon leaving the refugee camp of Récébédou on a Sunday, she went in search of a Mass. She was too late, so she knocked on a rectory door and asked the priest to give her communion, explaining why she was late. "You mean you went to see *those* people?" He refused her communion.[14]

While in Lyon she did, however, have the strength and support of a team, for she was one of the first members of *Amitié Chrétienne*.[15] This interreligious group had been formed for the express purpose of giving aid to Jews. It was composed of a small number of Protestants and Catholics who, working with some Jewish leaders, were dedicated to giving whatever help they could to the Jewish victims of Nazism and Vichy. With headquarters in Lyon, they were initially able to operate legally, providing food and medical supplies to the refugee camps. As the persecutions gained momentum the *Amitié Chrétienne* became involved in clandestine activities such as making and distributing false papers and getting people across the border into Switzerland.

The person most responsible for the production of false papers was Jean Stetten-Bernard, who met Germaine in the winter of 1941-42 at a seminar. Here is a description of her at that time: "Beneath the calm and composed appearance of this young woman he suspected a conviction, a passion, a willingness to fight, similar to his own."[16] She became one of the key members of the *Amitié*, undertaking some of its most dangerous tasks. When I asked her, "Were

13. Lyon, in the unoccupied zone (until November 1942) became the capital of Christian spiritual resistance.

14. Fleischner, in *Remembering for the Future*, p. 237.

15. Founded in 1940 by a group of Catholics to bring material assistance to Jews, the *Amitié Judéo-Chrétienne* soon grew into a joint Catholic, Protestant and Jewish effort involved in underground aid to Jews. It is alive and well today, an important instrument for Jewish-Christian dialogue in France.

16. Bédarida, *op. cit.*, p. 131.

you not afraid?" her answer was: "No. For me this was simply what had to be done, it was part of daily life in those days."[17]

One of those dangerous moments is referred to in Germaine's journal entry of February 4, 1943 (cf. above). It is also described more than once in discussions of the period that took place many years after the war. It was a moment of crisis in the history of the *Amitié* when, had it not been for the courage and presence of mind of a few, and a tardy intervention from the office of Cardinal Gerlier, the whole work of the *Amitié* might have come to an end. Here is a brief account of the crisis.

The Germans, breaking their promise, had invaded the unoccupied (or "free") zone on November 11, 1942 (cf. the journal), putting an end to whatever "freedom" had existed until then. On January 27, 1943 they invaded the offices of the *Amitié* in rue de Constantine in Lyon. All who were there were herded into one room, heated by a small stove, which gave off only a little heat. Under the pretext of stoking the fire one of their members managed to burn "under their very noses" some of the most incriminating papers. Fr. Chaillet, standing in a corner with his face against the wall, busily chewed and swallowed other papers.[18] A number of the core members were then taken to Gestapo headquarters. The police continued to occupy the offices, planning to make them into a trap in which other workers, unaware of what had happened, would be caught. How to prevent a total disaster and warn people? "A perfect strategy was worked out. Beginning at dawn the next day, Germaine Ribière, dressed as a cleaning woman, duly equipped with pail and brush, begins washing the stairs and floors of the offices for hours on end. Anyone coming

---

17. Interview with Eva Fleischner, taped, December 18, 1985.
18. Bédarida, *op. cit.*, p. 135.

to the door is warned by a slight movement of the hand to leave. Thus, one by one the visitors are warned by Germaine; not one of them fell into the trap."[19]

Germaine herself tells of her efforts after this arrest (cf. Feb. 4, 1943 above) to evacuate Jewish children with the help from the diocese. "We had children who had to be evacuated, more than a hundred of them, the *Amitié* was supposed to take care of them. Late in the evening – I had been running around all day – I went to the archdiocese to ask Cardinal Gerlier for help." She got only as far as his secretary: "The Cardinal already has enough such stories to worry about, I am sure he won't concern himself with this one." Germaine insisted that he telephone the Cardinal, "but (Gerlier) did not have time for me. Instead, he referred me to Dean Garraud, of the faculty of law and president of *Amitié*. Thanks to him, and the help of Pastor de Pury . . . the people who had been arrested were freed, and we were able to evacuate the children. . . . So in the end the Cardinal did help, but only when we pushed him against the wall."[20]

There were exceptions to this bleak array of unresponsiveness by the Roman Catholic hierarchy. Archbishop Saliége of Toulouse was for Germaine – and for many other members of the Christian Resistance – an unfailing support and source of strength. He was also the first to break the "wall of silence" and to issue a public protest against the deportations and inhuman treatment of Jews (cf. above, p. 88). Germaine speaks of him, to this day, with deep affection and respect.

---

19. *ibid.*, p. 136.
20. Ribière, in de Montclos, *op. cit.*, p. 205.

Germaine Ribière and the Rescue of Jews

For some French men and women the rescue of Jews was part of their resistance to Nazism, a patriotic duty. The Jews were the Nazis' most exposed victims; by helping them one was fighting France's enemy. For Germaine the rescue of Jews was a top priority.

"We knew what Nazism would do to the Jews, and that was my first reason for joining the Resistance. . . . I simply wanted to bear witness. . . ."[21] The matter-of-fact statement, "We knew what Nazism would do to the Jews," might lead one to think that the fate awaiting the Jews in France was self-evident to everyone. This was not the case. As we have seen, it took the deportations of the summer of 1942 to push some members of the hierarchy to speak out publicly against the persecution of Jews (cf. p. above). Father Lallier's comment, "Mademoiselle, I admire your charity . . . but we have our schools to worry about," appears more typical of the average French Catholic than Germaine's comment might lead one to think.

François Delpech, at the symposium already referred to, confirms that rescue of Jews was indeed of the utmost importance to Germaine, as it was for other members of the *Amitié Chrétienne*: "Concerning the help given to Jews, the most active members (of the *Amitié*) were Jean-Marie Soutou . . ., and a student from the women's branch of the J.E.C., Germaine Ribiére, who was as tireless as she was courageous. She constantly crisscrossed France to bring together the underground, visit camp internees, find or distribute information or funds." Referring to the Gestapo's occupation of the *Amitié's* offices on January 27, 1943 and the arrest of some of its leaders, Delpech speaks of Germaine "figuring out ways to hide Jews and get them into Switzerland."[22]

---

21. Taped interview with Eva Fleischner.

When I asked her how it was that she herself was never arrested her answer was: "I think it was simply because I lived all this as the life of everyday. I did what had to be done, but I was not rash or careless. I did not take useless risks, I was aware of the consequences. We had a work to do." "But were you not afraid?" "No, never. I always said: 'If someone in our network (of resistance) is afraid we must see to it that they take time out to rest, otherwise they will betray themselves. . . . I always slept well during the Occupation. There was nothing extraordinary about what I did, about the way I lived, during the war. I did what was required at the moment, and you simply face life as it comes. Nothing extraordinary about it. It was the Christian life of the moment. It was difficult, a challenge, but not extraordinary. . . ." That was not how others saw her. Looking back to those years, Henri de Lubac told me, "We called her our Joan of Arc."[23]

An important and urgent aspect of Germaine's work on behalf of Jews was bringing relief to those interned in the camps of the "free" zone. The conditions in these camps were wretched, the prisoners lacked the most basic necessities and lived in filth (cf. the Journal, August 31, 1941). Germaine laments the absence of a Catholic presence in the camps, but she and some other members of the *Amitié* did what they could to help. Vichy, worried about arousing the anger of the local rural population if they ever knew the true condition of the camps and of the deportations to the East, was in the habit of throwing up a smoke screen. Whenever an "operation" took place, they made sure that social workers were on hand, ostensibly to see to it that the prisoners were treated humanely. Furthermore – again

---

22. In de Montclos, *op. cit.*, p. 163.
23. Cardinal Henri de Lubac, S.J., to Eva Fleischner, interview, Paris, October 1, 1985.

to reassure the local population – these social workers were
to be chosen from respected families in the region. We shall
let Germaine speak in her own words:[24]

> It is difficult to imagine today the spirit of national
> abdication and perversion with which these camps
> were organized. I knew several camps personally, es-
> pecially one of them near Limoges, in which I had lived
> for a long time. This is what happened. It was August
> 1942, the time of the great round ups. I had just returned
> home from being in charge of a J.E.C. camp. My mother
> told me that I should immediately go and see the rabbi,
> who needed my help. . . . I went to see Rabbi Deutsch.
> He had just learned that the arrests of foreign Jews were
> about to take place. The director of the National Social
> Services *(Secours National)* had come to tell him that they
> were going to put social workers into the camps in-
> tended for foreign Jews, to organize efforts to help. In
> reality, all they cared about was to keep up appearances,
> so that they could say that social workers were looking
> after the prisoners – never mind what was really hap-
> pening. The man was trying to find the right people,
> they had to be from "good" families. Rabbi Deutsch told
> him he thought he could find someone – he was think-
> ing of me. My family was Christian, we had a good
> reputation in town.

> The director agreed that I go. The colonel in charge of
> the whole affair told me: "Tomorrow morning, starting
> at 4 a.m., we'll arrest all foreign Jews, around 800
> people. We'll bring them together on the *Place de la
> Poste*, then we'll take them to the camp by bus. We'll
> try to 'soften' things, but these are our orders." He was
> very pleased with the way he had planned everything.
> I left him saying, "I promise you that I shall work as a
> Christian, and as a French woman." Then I hurried to
> find any Jewish representatives I knew and we went

---

24. Ribière, in de Montclos, *op. cit.*, p. 206f.

everywhere telling people, "Leave, don't remain at home, hide!" The next morning, instead of 800 people they found only 29. The authorities wondered what had happened, but they never caught on.

Together with a friend, Hélène Durand, whose father was a doctor in Limoges, Germaine entered the camp and lived there for a time, going in and out each day and passing on information and papers, while Hélène, who spoke German, remained in the camp.

That round up was only the beginning. Eventually nearly all who had been able to escape initially were caught. "Thinking the danger had passed they came back home and were caught. In the end they were all deported, all alike, of course in cattle cars."[25]

"There were scenes of desperation everywhere. The doomed prisoners had begged me to accompany them, and I had promised to do so – to remain with them until the moment they were handed over to the Germans. In order to get on the train I had borrowed a Red Cross uniform. But the morning of departure, at the station of Limoges, a representative of the Red Cross ordered me to get off the train. I refused. At Châteauroux a French lieutenant ordered me off the train. I refused. He tried again at Bierzon, at the moment they were sealing the cars hermetically, having removed sanitary facilities – it was all the more dreadful because people were suffering from dysentry. I went to the German officer in charge to protest. The French lieutenant saw me talking with him, came up and told the German officer: 'Ask to see her papers and arrest her, her papers are not in order.' The German . . . let me go, but I was stopped soon after by the same lieutenant. You see the kind of French people we were!"

---

25. *ibid.*

"That wasn't the end. When I came back to Limoges I was asked to appear before the head of the Red Cross, because I had done something illegal, and was told to apologize [she refused]. The director in charge of the National Social Service, who had agreed to my working inside the camp and was unaware of what I planned to do, had also told me not to accompany the convoy. I ran into him later and he told me: 'I agree with you, but I can't say so, because it would mean difficulties with the authorities.'" And she concludes: "This was the climate, not only in Lyon, Paris, or Limoges, but nearly everywhere in France. . . ."[26]

It is striking that, in this vivid account recalled years later, Germaine continues to include herself as a potential victimizer. "You see the kind of French people we were!" One might expect her to say "they" rather than "we," since she is referring to people like the French lieutenant who tried to keep her from helping the victims. She does not, however, make the clear-cut distinction between him and herself one would expect. The "we" is an expression of her deep sense of solidarity – not only with the suffering victims, but with the sins and failures of her people, whether in her church or her country. It is, I believe, one of the most extraordinary characteristics of this woman, and it permeates her journal. "I am afraid that one of these days, when we wake up, it will be too late and we shall all have become Nazis" (May 27, 1949). She herself was awake, but the country was asleep – and this involved her also. And again: "We say that we believe in Christ, that we love him, yet we allow him to be despised" (March 25, 1942), etc. Just as the suffering of the Jews is for her part of the suffering of all humanity, so too the sins of the bystanders and perpetrators are the sins of all humanity, including herself.

---

26. *ibid.*

Yet she refused to judge, to condemn, to hate. "I saw things that ought to have scandalized me to the bottom of my soul" (she is referring to visiting Dachau at the end of the war). "But there was only human misery. The human being is weak, miserable, sinful. And I am called to enter into this misery, into this sin. . . . When I was refused communion I could have been scandalized; instead, I wept."[27] She refused to hate. "In the presence of hatred I feel an icy chill . . ., it is not the world of God, it is the refusal of God. . . . I wept at what I found in Dachau. . . . It is the anti-world. . . . I must fight against it . . . with my whole self, with my whole life. . . ."[28]

Hers was a life rooted in a deep Christian faith. When I asked her what kept her from leaving the church, the passivity and failure of which she saw so clearly, and what sustained her in her faith, she answered simply: "Christ. I come from a region of France where there are vineyards. When I read in the gospel Jesus' parable of the vine and the branches I understood. I knew what a vine is, the analogy was perfect for me. Humanity is the body of Christ. I felt as if I were holding the vine and the branches in my hand. . . . How could I have denied this relationship?"[29]

She speaks of the deep formative influence on her life of the atmosphere that permeated her home, and of her mother in particular. "My mother raised us to have respect for life, to marvel at life, at all life. . . . Our house was always open to everyone. Whenever someone was in trouble they would come to see my mother, even in the middle of the night." During the war Germaine, the youngest of three children, was the only one at home, and she was rarely there. Yet her mother never tried to hold her

---

27. Conversation with Eva Fleischner.
28. *ibid.*
29. Quoted in Fleischner, n. 1 above, p. 236.

back: "I know you are needed, go, don't worry about me."
Worn out by the hardships of the war her mother died in
1943. Her brother, a seminarian, had been taken to Germany for forced labor; her sister and husband were in
North Africa during the war.

Germaine's grief over her mother's death was intensified by the fact that the diocese sent no representative to
the funeral – as would have been customary in the case
where a family member was a priest or seminarian. "Because we were not for Vichy," was her answer to my question. The house was taken over by the Gestapo the day of
the funeral, "We had been denounced."[30]

Germaine says little of these deep personal sorrows.
It is as if they merge with the ocean of misery of the war
years.

A brief note about her life after the war.

Given her prominence in the Resistance it would have
been easy for her to stay on in an important post at the
moment of Liberation – she was urged to do so. "Only until
the last prisoner is returned home," was her reply. She felt
called to resume and complete her studies, even though
she had no money and her home was gone. "When I handed
in my resignation people told me, 'You are crazy to give
up your position!' I answered, "I am not made for this sort
of thing.' At that moment, being faithful meant for me to
resume my studies. . . ."[31]

Being faithful: it is a phrase that recurred frequently
in our conversations. "I think I understood in those days
that I could not *not* be faithful. No matter what the cost . . . .
When one has touched life at such a depth, when one has
seen such destruction. . . . Not to be faithful would be to
lie to oneself. Inconsistency is not possible. Either the Gos-

---

30. Conversation with Eva Fleischner.
31. *ibid.*

pel is life, or it is not. 'Whoever says he/she loves God and
does not love his/her brother or sister is a liar.' We are
miserable sinners, yes. But this fundamental refusal –
No."[32] Is this, perhaps, one of the keys to who this woman
is?

　　Germaine Ribière's commitment to Jews and Judaism,
and to the State of Israel, continues to this day. She had
met Fr. Roger Braun, S.J., during the war, in 1941, when he
came to her home to ask for false papers. "Mother took one
look at him and said, 'he won't make it through the war,'
he looked so ill. I knew him through Cardinal Saliège." She
began working with him in the camps, where he was chaplain. When, in 1967, he founded the journal *Rencontre*[33]
Germaine became one of its editors and contributors, and
after Fr. Braun's death assumed the chief responsibilitiy
for the journal. In the fall of 1985, when hardly anyone as
yet had heard of the Carmelite convent at Auschwitz, she
brought news of it to Cardinal Lustiger of Paris at the end
of one of her trips to Poland. The drawn-out controversy
that followed is history, and belongs to another chapter.[34]

---

32. *ibid.*
33. *Rencontre. Chrétiens et Juifs.* Revue trimestrielle. 82 issues were published
　　between 1967 and 1986.
34. A useful compendium of this controversy is found in *Memory Offended*,
　　edited by Carol Rittner and John Roth. New York: Praeger, 1991.

Chapter Five

Marie-Rose Gineste: The Woman With a Bicycle

I HAD FOUND REFERENCES TO MARIE-ROSE GINESTE IN A number of books and documents relating to the French resistance and rescue of Jews. They always appeared in the same context: she was the social worker to whom Bishop Théas of Montauban had turned in August 1942 for help in distributing his letter of protest concerning Vichy's anti-Jewish measures throughout his diocese. What had led her to assume this important role, I wondered. Hoping to find out I visited her in October 1985, in the apartment where she lived since 1937 with her mother, until the latter's death.

I was received with great warmth, and with joy. I was the first American, it turned out, to visit her since the end of the war – she had hidden several American pilots. With pride she showed me a letter of recognition and thanks from General Eisenhower, beautifully framed. And, in the best French tradition, she had prepared a festive meal for me. We talked for several hours, over a bottle of good wine. This first visit was followed by others over the years. On two occasions I was an overnight guest in her home – the small apartment with a large, enchanting garden hidden in the back. The account that follows is based on our many conversations, on letters and documents she sent me (she never failed to respond to a question), and on material published in a variety of sources.[1]

Marie-Rose Gineste was born in 1911, in a small village not far from Montauban. Her parents were peasants who worked the land, and she too worked in the fields, attending school only until the age of twelve. "They were Catholics, but not as religious as I am today." When she was twenty a terrible flood devastated the village, killing many people. She then moved, with her mother, to neighboring Montauban. There she worked for some time as a seamstress, then for the diocese. At the time of France's defeat in May-June 1940 she was working at the diocesan office for social affairs.

She recalls the chaotic weeks that followed the defeat, when Montauban, like other cities in the south, was flooded with refugees: soldiers as well as civilians, on foot, on bicycles, in trucks. One Sunday she set out to visit her sister in her native village, and found it almost impossible to cross to the other side of the road on her bicycle, because the road was clogged with refugees.

Then came the armistice, followed by General de Gaulle's appeal to France of June 18. "What an immense hope was born in me – as in many others – when I heard this appeal from General de Gaulle as I listened to the BBC (which I did regularly). France was not finished after all, a general asked us to continue the fight! His challenge echoed my own deepest feelings, and in my heart I pledged him my allegiance. I had yet to discover how I could translate my commitment into concrete action, that came later."[2]

---

1. See, among others; Renée Bédarida, *Les Armes de l'Esprit: Témoignage Chrétien (1941-1944)*. Paris: Les Editions Ouvrières, 1977. Eva Fleischner, "Can the Few become the Many? Some Catholics in France who saved Jews during the Holocaust," in *Remembering for the Future*, Vol. I, p. 233ff. Oxford: Pergamon Press, 1989. Marie-Rose Gineste, unpublished *Mémoire*. Montauban, 1974. Gay Block and Malka Drucker, *Rescuers. Portraits of Moral Courage in the Holocaust*. New York and London: Holmes & Meier, 1992, pp. 128 ff. Mordecai Paldiel, *The Path of the Righteous*. Hoboken, N.J.: KTAV, 1993. Susan Zuccotti, *The Holocaust, the French, and the Jews*. Basic Books, 1993.

She speaks of the awareness she and others in Montauban had of being privileged because they were spared the suffering of those in the north. This awareness gave birth to their sense of obligation to do whatever they could to help. Marie-Rose and her mother gave up their bedroom to a soldier, and during one month lived in a damp, dark room of their small apartment. Under the leadership of Bishop Théas the secretariat for social affairs, along with other Catholic organizations, gave whatever help it could to the refugees from the north.

In September 1941 Marie-Rose and a friend, Mlle. M. Colombani, were asked by the founders of *Témoignage Chrétien* to assume responsibility for distributing the underground periodical that had just been launched.[3] Both women took on this task with enthusiasm. Their role was to organize and carry out the distribution of *Témoignage Chrétien*, and later of the *Courrier* as well. The entire stock of publications would be brought to Marie-Rose's apartment by a member of the Resistance. From there the women delivered it to various people known to be working in the Resistance, or who were sympathizers. After July 1942 Marie-Rose carried out this task herself. In August of that same summer events took place that were to make her famous, to this day, in the annals of the French resistance to the Nazis and the rescue attempts on behalf of Jews.

The context for these events was the change in public opinion in general, and in the Catholic hierarchy in particular, that was caused by the deportations of Jews throughout France that summer. Voices of protest now began to be heard, among them some belonging to the leaders of the Catholic Church (cf. pp. 72 and 73 above). Let us repeat here the prophetic statement issued by Bishop

---

2. *Mémoire*, p. 3.
3. See n. (10) in Ch. Four.

Pierre-Marie Théas of Montauban, Marie-Rose's home diocese:

> . . . . I must make heard the indignant protest of the Christian conscience, and I proclaim that all people, aryan or non-aryan, are brothers [and sisters], because all are created by the same God: that all, whatever their race or religion, are entitled to respect from individuals and the state. The current anti-semitic measures are in contempt of human dignity, a violation of the most sacred rights of the individual and the family. . . .[4]

The bishop then asked Marie-Rose, whom he knew to be active in the Resistance, if she would be willing to type and duplicate his letter so that it could be read in the parishes of the diocese on the following Sunday, August 30. The young social worker was glad to help. When she asked Bishop Théas how he planned to distribute the letter and he replied, by mail, she commented that the censors would not let it pass, and suggested instead that she herself undertake to bring the letter to all the churches of the diocese. Bishop Théas accepted her offer. Starting early the next morning Marie-Rose took her bicycle, and for three days delivered the letter to every parish, crisscrossing the country "like a modern Paul Revere."[5] She made only one exception: a priest who was known for his collaborationist attitude – "he never saved a single life, and after the war he saved himself only by disappearing from the diocese!"

The following Sunday the bishop's letter was read from every pulpit during Mass, with the authorities having no idea as to how each parish had obtained the document. Marie-Rose tells how, in her joy at having played a role in this subversive activity, she attended all the Masses in the Montauban cathedral that Sunday morning, to hear the letter read again and again.

---

4. See also p. 73 above.
5. Paldiel, *op. cit.*, p. 25.

From that time on Bishop Théas asked her to be responsible for finding hiding places for Jewish children and adults, and for providing them with false identity cards. "Until October 1943 I obtained false papers and ration cards through various friends in the Resistance. After that date we fabricated them ourselves, turning them over to Bishop Théas and Jewish friends in the Resistance. . . ."[6]

More than forty years had passed since those clandestine activities. When we met in the fall of 1985 her hair was white, she was in her seventies. The famous bicycle was the first thing I saw in the front hall of her home. It looked a little older and more tired, but was still serviceable, she still rode it daily to her office. Although long past retirement age she felt unable to refuse when the chancery asked her help (she still works there nine years later, now in her eighties).

For a short time after the war Marie-Rose served as Mayor of Montauban. Then, for many years, she was a member of the city's municipal council, and administrator of social security. She has received many honors for her work. On July 14, 1974 she was inducted into the Legion of Honor, France's highest distinction. Her favorite is the Military Medal of the Resistance, "only forty women in France have received it."[7] But more precious than all others, to her, is Yad Vashem's Medal for the Righteous Among the Nations, which she received in the spring of 1986. Her journey to Israel on that occasion remains a high point of her life and the realization of a dream. When she planted her tree at Yad Vashem she was surrounded by a group of French Jews whom she had helped during the war. And she told me how one day a taxi came to her hotel in Jerusalem and drove her, over many miles, to the home of Mme.

---

6. Gineste, *Mémoire*.
7. Block and Drucker, *Rescuers*, p. 131.

Emilie Braun, now 88 years old, for whom she had found
a hiding place with the farmers in the region near Montauban, and who thus was able to survive the war.

On the occasion of receiving the National Order of
Merit M. Achille Teste, a former prisoner in Buchenwald,
drew this profile of her in his speech: "From a rural milieu,
solid from every point of view – physically, morally, intel-
lectually, temperamentally. A deep faith. A lively intelli-
gence. Also great sensitivity, without the least trace of
egoism. She had a kind way of looking at people, which
often inspired hope and trust in the many under-
priviledged ones she has hepled over her long years of
apostolate. . . ."[8] Before concluding he read a message from
Bishop Théas, now bishop of Lourdes:

> . . . . I greatly rejoice in the distinction which the gov-
> ernment is bestowing on Marie-Rose Gineste. . . . It will
> be a modest tribute from her country toward a French
> woman who found in her Christian faith. . . . the in-
> domitable courage to resist the oppression of the occu-
> pying power. Please convey to Marie-Rose Gineste the
> great esteem, affection and admiration I have for her.

When, in the fall of 1993, I wrote to her to ask for the
title of the *Mémoire* she had given me on the occasion of
our first meeting she replied: "The *Mémoire* to which you
refer had no title. . . . If you like, here is what you might
say with reference to this account of the years when France
was vanquished, under Nazi occupation, years lived by a
French woman who seemed hardly predestined for the
work she did from 1940 to 1944: 'A very humble young
woman, having fully understood the situation of her country, she worked for the liberation of France without counting the cost.'" And she added: "I wish to stress that I am

---

8. Montauban, October 28, 1967; text sent to me by Marie-Rose Gineste.

no intellectual, that I went to school only until the age of twelve."[9]

We shall conclude this account of Marie-Rose Gineste's rescue activities on behalf of Jews with the last words of her *Mémoire* (p. 48). They answer, in part, the question posed early in this chapter: What led her to assume the role she played during the war years?

> I have probably forgotten some facts and events, never mind. I think I have spoken of the main ones in the preceding pages. What matters is not to talk about them, but to have lived them, to have acted as I did during that period of underground struggle, during those four years which were a high point of my life. I believe I may say that during those years my actions were ordinary ones, actions of every day, and that I never refused any service the Resistance asked of me.
>
> My commitment, my actions, were in no way motivated by hatred. I do not think I ever felt hate toward anyone.
>
> From the first day to the last I did what I did because of my Christian faith. It is this faith which has, ever since my childhood, ruled and guided my whole life; also during the war, during the Occupation, and since then, until today . . . in all my various and many commitments, and in my daily life.
>
> Montauban, June 12, 1974

---

9. Marie-Rose Gineste in a letter to Eva Fleischner, November 24, 1993.

Chapter Six

Germaine Bocquet: The Woman Who Hid Jules Isaac

GERMAINE WAS TWENTY-ONE YEARS OLD WHEN THE WAR broke out. By 1941 she had become part of the resistance network of Edmond Michelet in Brive where, in the fall of that year, her main task was to obtain false papers for people in danger and to hide Jewish children whose parents had been deported.[1] The following summer she was busy helping Jewish families cross the border into Switzerland. On one of those trips she met a young resistance worker engaged in the same kind of work, Jacques Bocquet. They continued their underground activities after their marriage in January 1943. In the fall of that year Germaine met Jules Isaac, the distinguished French historian, who was to spend a year with the young couple hiding from the Gestapo, and who became a deep and permanent influence in their lives. In this chapter we shall focus on Germaine's early years, which help explain why this young woman became involved in the rescue of Jews. Because of Isaac's crucial importance for Jewish-Christian relations in the years since Vatican-II, we shall also speak of those of his experiences

---

1. Edmond Michelet was one of the first to recognize the perils of fascism, he issued a call to resist even before DeGaulle's appeal. His home in Brive became a center of resistance already at the beginning of the war. Later deported to Dachau he survived the war to become minister in the French government. His home in Brive is now the Edmond Michelet Museum, supervised by his widow and children. The story of his imprisonment in Dauchau is told by him in the book *Rue de la Liberté*.

prior to and during the war which eventually led him to his life's work: the study of Christian antisemitism.

Early Childhood[2]

Germain's mother died when she was two years old. The child was raised by her father, Lucien Chantrenne, a brilliant, highly educated man, lover of the classics. He had been a classmate of Léon Blum at the Ecole Normale Supérieure. From a deeply anti-clerical milieu – his mother, a public school teacher, had little use for the church – M. Chantrenne had become an atheist. "We had every kind of newspaper and magazine at home, but religious publications were forbidden," Germaine was to say many years later. Her early years were lived in a vibrant intellectual atmosphere devoid of all religion. "Maybe I was fortunate. Had I grown up in a traditional Cathloic milieu I might have encountered antisemitism."[3]

When Germaine was eight years old her father decided to have her baptized, despite his aversion to religion "for social reasons. He thought it would increase my chances of a good marriage later." Along with baptism came three years of obligatory religious instruction, to which he agreed as a matter of honor. Little did he suspect what those three years would come to mean in his young daughter's life.

First encounter with Catholicism

The catechist who was in charge of the religion classes in Germaine's school was a young woman then in her early

---

2. See also Eva Fleischner, "Can the Few become the Many? Some Catholics in France who saved Jews during the Holocaust." Paper given at Oxford, at the international symposium "Remembering for the Future," July 1988, published in *Remembering for the Future*, Oxford and New York: Pergamon Press, 1989. Vol. I, pp. 233-247.

3. Conversation with Eva Fleischner, August 10, 1988, unpublished tape.

twenties by the name of Françoise Derkenne. (She was to become, after World War II, one of the leaders of the catechetical renewal in the French Church.) In an interview in 1986 Françoise Derkenne recalled her years as a young catechist.[4] Biblical studies for lay Catholics, especially for women, were unknown in the 1920's and 1930's. But she told her children of the great biblical figures, beginning with Abraham, as she prepared them for Christmas. Asked if she was aware at the time of Christian antisemitism her answer was: "No. I came from a deeply Christian family, there was no antisemitism at home. And my love of philosophy had always caused me to approach my faith critically. I simply discarded any elements that seemed distorted or harmful to me."[5]

The young teacher's influence on the children was profound, as was that of the school chaplain, a priest from the local parish. Germaine recalls him as a "saintly man" who not only taught the children catechism, but initiated them into the life of prayer and of the spirit. "I remember how we not only recited our prayers, but we began to have an experience of God."[6]

The catechism taught was that of the diocese of Paris and, like all catechisms at the time, consisted of questions and answers. In Germaine's school, however, everything was commented on, explained, related to the Sunday's Gospel and the Bible. "Everything was alive, we learned the sacred history of the Bible. . . . The Jews were for us the people who gave us Jesus."[7]

Those three years marked the child so deeply that when they came to an end and her father told her, "At last

---

4. Derkenne, conversation with Eva Fleischner, Paris, August 16, 1986.
5. *ibid.*
6. Bocquet, conversation with Eva Fleischner, August 10, 1986.
7. *ibid.*

you are done with all that nonsense!" she replied, "Oh no, Papa, it has only just begun!"[8] Behind her fathers back she started going to daily Mass and continued her religious education throughout high school. Her memories of that time are still vivid.

High school years

"I had to hide my going to Mass from my father, otherwise there would have been dreadful scenes at home. I used to take an earlier train to school so that I could skip my breakfast and fast – we had to fast before Mass in those days. Maybe in the end it was a very healthy education in the faith because it obliged us to stand on our own two feet, to come to a personal faith. There was no family you could count on, though we did have our Catholic youth group.

"Perhaps temperament and age also played a role. As an adolescent you tend to go against your family's norms. Perhaps, if I had come from a religious, traditional family I might have reacted in the other direction. As it was it all came together for me: formation in prayer, which gave me an inner strength, and perhaps, at the purely human level, opposition to what my father wanted. . . . "[9]

She recalls other memories of her spiritual life during her high school years in Versailles. "We formed our own little support group of pious young girls, to help each other pray. We called ourselves 'the little friends of Jesus!' . . . We took turns praying the rosary in the train from Paris to Versailles. After class we used to go to a small chapel to pray; we read *The Imitation of Christ* on the way there. At first we were a bit isolated in our own small world, but we soon made contact with the J.E.O. (the Young Christian

---

8. *ibid.*

9. *ibid.*

Workers, a Catholic youth movement). This meant we had study groups at school with the chaplain; meditations on the Gospel, involvement with the lay apostolate. . . . So, between the ages of 12 and 17, no more catechism, but a spiritual formation that helped us deepen in faith. We even had religious discussions with some of our professors. We proudly wore our J.E.O. badge, although we were not supposed to wear badges of any kind. I admit we were a bit over-zealous, we could have been more discreet! But what is really quite amazing is that several of our classmates converted and were baptized at the age of 16 or 17 – girls from irreligious families like my own asked to be baptized."

As to antisemitism, she encountered it neither at home nor in school. She had no interest in history – "I am ashamed to say it, I ought to have known something about the Dreyfus Affair. But history didn't interest me at all." [Her meeting with Jules Isaac during the war was to change this.] "What did interest me, passionately, was mathematics, and poetry."[10]

The impression that is conveyed by these recollections is that of a young woman of deep, traditional piety, a piety rooted not in her home and family, but in a sound religious education at school. Neither at home nor in school did she encounter antisemitism.

The Meeting with Jules Isaac

The Resistance network in Brive decided to disperse in November 1943, because the situation had become too dangerous. Germaine and Jacques now moved in with Germaine's grandmother, who lived in an isolated corner of France, the Berry. One day Germaine was contacted by a teacher from the neighboring village and asked if they would take in a man whose family had been arrested and

---

10. *ibid.*

who was himself being sought by the Gestapo. She readily agreed (Jacques was away on a mission at the time). She was asked to meet the stranger in Clermond-Ferrand, in the house of friends. She told him of the primitive circumstances of the life that would be his if he came to live with them: an old farmhouse in the middle of nowhere, no running water – "We drew the water from a well and chopped our own wood for the stove. He was undeterred, and insisted on telling me who he was. I did not need or want to know – his being a hunted man was enough for me. But he insisted: 'Did you go to high school?' 'Yes.' 'What was your history text?' 'Malet and Isaac.' 'Well I am Jules Isaac.' And that is how the one who was to become 'the uncle' for us entered our lives; not only thanks to false papers, but also thanks to the affection which very soon bound us together."[11]

His false papers made him M. Jean Breton, retired, born in Valenciennes (Jacques' family came from there and Isaac knew the town, having lived there for a time). Then Germaine returned to Issoudum and waited for him. Together they went to the old farmhouse in Prault, lost in the deserted plain, surrounded by farm buildings and a large garden, where her grandmother had retired. Again Isaac insisted on revealing his identity to the old lady. In her eighties now, a former school teacher in the village, she was deeply embarrassed to be able to offer this famous man only such simple lodgings. But her guest's simplicity – he willingly participated in household chores – quickly put her at ease, and "she was to do the impossible to make 'Monsieur Jean's stay with us as comfortable as possible.' "

Because of the importance of Jules Isaac to Jewish-Christian dialogue today, as well as to Germaine's life, let

---

11. The story of Jules Isaac's stay with the young couple is told by Germaine Bocquet in *Dans l'Amitié de Jules Isaac*, No. 3, 1981.

us at this point give a brief sketch of this remarkable man in the years preceding and during the war. We are able to let him speak for himself much of the time, thanks to a text by Isaac himself.[12]

Jules Isaac

Before the war Jules Isaac's name had come to be known to every high school teacher and student in France as the author of the history textbook series, Malet-Isaac, which was used in schools throughout France. Albert Malet, the original author, had been killed in World War I without being able to complete the last volume. In 1923 Isaac, then a history teacher, was asked by the publisher to write the last chapter.

Reform in the school curriculum eventually required an entirely new program, and Isaac was asked to assume this responsibility. "With some hesitation," he writes, not without irony, "due perhaps to my biblical name, little suited to wide popularity." He also had not attended one of France's prestigious schools, like Malet and the publisher himself, "and it took the latter some time to admit that, however regrettably, one might nonetheless not be lacking in knowledge or even talent which can, after all, grow in any soil!" (p. 4). And so the series Malet-Isaac was born.

Isaac's main reason for accepting this arduous assignment, which occupied him for seven long years, was the opportunity it provided to influence French youth. "After all, why not write a text that is thoughtful, balanced, based on careful documentation, one that raises burning contemporary issues?" (such as the Franco-German war of 1870,

---

12. Jules Isaac, *Survol en Guis d'Introduction*, published in *Les Cahiers du Sud*, 1964. Our reference is a xeroxed copy of twelve pages, inscribed in Isaac's own hand "for Germaine and Jacques Bocquet, their adopted uncle." Page references are to this text.

where he included excerpts from a respected German source).

This work greatly broadened his authority and scope as educator. In 1936 he was named chief inspector of high school education for all of France, and once again revised the series, now under his own name. Its legendary success continued into the postwar years. Little did he suspect that, although he was approaching sixty, his real life's work lay still ahead.

Throughout the thirties Isaac had been aware of the gathering storm. He had tried, in vain, to alert his compatriots to the danger of facism, through conferences, articles, and contact with German scholars. "I foresaw the catastrophe. . . . , and was willing to risk everything to turn away the mortal danger . . . We were still debating Munich 1938 when the war broke out, precipitating us into a demonic future" (p. 6).

"Shall I ever be able to speak of this last, this most cruel stage of my life, in which I touched the unspeakable?" (*ibid.*). "I had expected too much of my country. Suddenly, brutally, it was made clear to me that, in order to be considered . . . a good Frenchman, it was not enough to have been one, fully, totally, all my life. In addition one had to be recognized as such not only by the all-conquering enemy, but by one's own people, many of whom – officials with Marshal Pétain at their head and Maurras[13] as their spiritual director – seemed all too ready to follow the example set by the enemy in their fierce antisemitism. . . . Thus it was that, beginning in October 1941, through [anti-Jewish] legislation, we were disenfranchised, thrown into a new, infamous category as contagious vermin, as lepers, without recourse, exposed to all that human malice and

---

13. See n. (3), ch. Four.

cowardice can devise. Rich fruit of Franco-Nazi collaboration, for which some still hunger today.

"Impossible to stop half-way on such a slope. We
know today where this voyage into the night was to lead:
logically, inexorably, to Auschwitz. . . . The abyss had
opened before me like a sudden, terrible crack in the earth's
surface, in the sinister hours of May-June 1940. Yet I was
not precipated into it immediately, but in stages. It took
three years before I was to touch its depths" (p. 7).

The stages referred to are three places to which Isaac
moved with his family. Denounced by a collaborator in
late 1940 they fled from Paris to Vichy. Isaac's son-in-law
had taken a post in the Vichy government which served
him as cover for his Resistance activities. For a while Isaac
was stillable to retain his position, though he writes that
he was a marked man now, whom many of his colleages
began to shun. After October 1941 he became an outcast.

The family then decided to move to Aix-en-Provence
(Isaac was to settle there after the war for the rest of his
life) where, surrounded by his family and the great natural
beauty of the country, he again found a measure of peace.
"They could rob me of my civil rights, of all my privileges
and titles, but not of my being, not of my soul. I remained
the one I had always been."

The third stage came with the German invasion of the
"free"zone in November 1942. The family now sought refuge in the Haute-Loire. What sustained Isaac during this
time was his family, still intact, and his work. This had,
however, taken a wholly new direction.

Through his experience of persecution Isaac had become more and more preoccupied with the Jewish question. "It haunted my mind while Jewish solidarity haunted
my heart and conscience" (p. 8). "I was part of this people
Israel that was hated, calumniated, despised. It was time
to wage a new battle, to get to the root of the evils imposed

on us. Despite the obvious racism [of the Nazis], this evil was rooted in a thousand-year-old tradition, a Christian – or rather pseudo-Christian – tradition. For one had only to read the Gospels, to read them attentively, to become convinced that this tradition deformed both the scriptural and historical truth. This is what I wanted to show clearly. Starting early in 1943 I began work on *Jesus and Israel*.[14] The depths of the Jewish roots of the Gospel message, and of Christian antisemitism, were for me a daily, and increasingly overwhelming discovery. I was called to transmit this discovery to all whose hearts were open to receive it"(p. 8).

And so it was that Jules Isaac's life's work was born, in the midst of a hunted, nomadic existence in occupied France. The man whose name had been a household word for many years throughout France as author of one of the most successful textbook series was to become known, after the war and far beyond the borders of France, as the author of two ground-breaking studies on Christian antisemitism, and of the term, "the Teaching of Contempt."

This new work would eventually lead Isaac to Rome where, in an audience with Pope John XXIII in 1960 he persuaded the pope to put the question of the Church and the Jewish people on the agenda of the Council that John had recently announced. Isaac's moving account of his meeting with the pope, and with Cardinal Bea, is told in the last page of the *Survey* on which we have drawn here (p. 12). It takes us, however, beyond the war years and his refuge with Germaine Bocquet's family, to which we shall now return.

---

14. *Jesus and Israel*. New York: Holt, Rinehart and Winston 1971; original French edition 1959.

Hiding from the Gestapo

"I was making slow progress in this work [on *Jesus and Israel*], for which I was poorly prepared, when there burst upon me the terrible storm which was to devastate my life forever"(p. 8). Instead of hiding in the woods Isaac and his wife decided to move to Riom, in the plane, to be closer to their children and to libraries. "We had hardly settled down when the Gestapo descended on us – first in Vichy on my son-in-law, pure 'aryan' but member of the Resistance, and my daughter and younger son, then, in Riom, on us." (Isaac's older son Daniel was with DeGaulle's forces in North Africa.) "I was the only one of the five who escaped, through a bizarre incident . . . There now began for me a life lived completely underground. More leprous than ever, condemned to death. . . . , I found in the Resistance help, friendship, and as it were a new family. Taken to a corner of the Berry I became the adopted 'uncle' of those who had agreed to take me in, so intimately that I remain their 'uncle' to this day . . . " (p. 9).

The chance incident which saved Isaac from the Gestapo when his wife was taken was indeed "bizarre": he was getting a haircut when the Gestapo came. His initial reaction upon finding his wife gone was one of desperation. He presented himself at police headquarters, so that he could join her in whatever lay ahead. It was supper time, the office was about to close, and he was told to come back the next morning. During the night friends convinced him that his arrest would not save his family; moreover, he had a work to do. He must go into hiding. A week later he met Germaine Bocquet.

And now there began for Isaac the life of a hermit. No other house within two miles; the plain stretched to infinity, desolate in the cold of winter. Few contacts with the outside world. Germaine's husband put in only brief appearances between his resistance missions. From time to time a teacher-friend visited, bringing mail, an underground newspaper, and news from the BBC, which Germaine could not get on their old, "sputtering" radio.

The evenings were more lively. In the neighboring farmhouse a Hungarian Jewish engineer had taken refuge, disguised as a farmhand. Germaine writes of him: "Strange farmhand! The people on the farm called him 'the student' because the walls of his room were lined with books. Every evening, his work finished, Paul Stern joined us and there began endless discussions. In this committed Marxist, in this vibrant yet caustic revolutionary, gifted with a vast political and historical culture, Jules Isaac found a partner whom he never tired of challenging. A deep mutual respect was born between these two passionate, generous men. The evenings with Paul were a source of comfort and energy for Isaac.

"But his real comfort and reason for living was the work into which he threw himself the moment he came to us. He asked me for books, but all I had was a Bible and daily missal." Fortunately, thanks to the kindness of a priest of the Sacred Heart in Issoudum, Fr. Klein, Germaine was able to make regular trips to the library of the convent there, always equipped with a list of books Isaac needed. Whenever he could Fr. Klein brought the books himself. The friendship he formed with Isaac lasted throughout the family's stay in the Berry.[15]

The work Isaac was so passionately engaged in was the first revisions of the manuscript that was to become *Jesus and Israel*. "He spoke to me often and at some length about his work, the importance of which, I must confess, I did not at first understand. For me antisemitism was part of Nazi racist ideology, and I had no idea that it could have roots in Christian teaching. What he told me did not fit

---

15. See n. (11) above.

into my own religious upbringing. . . . The religious education I had received . . . left in my soul nothing but respect and gratitude for the Jewish people who had given to the world the prophets, the Virgin Mary, Christ, and the apostles. I knew them only as people of the convenant and promise. . . . , the people from whom came the Messiah. . . . , a people to whom he belonged in every aspect of his life. . . . I had never heard of Jews as 'Christ-killers', only that it was our sins that had crucified Jesus, from which his passion and death had redeemed us. . . . Moreover, in my youth, and especially during the period of Occupation, I had met nothing but devotion to and friendship for the many Jews who were being persecuted. Never any antisemitism.

"I told him all this, and he listened with grave attention and sympathy, though also with some skepticism. When he learned that my teacher had been a friend of the Maritains the puzzle was resolved. . . . "[16]

Germaine's conversations with Isaac as he worked on his book were the young woman's first encounter with Christian antisemitism:

> He made me read the texts he was collecting. Many were terrible in their virulent hatred of Jews. And they were the work of famous Christian theologians – Catholic, Protestant, and Orthodox! I was stunned to learn how many texts from scripture had been used to create a climate of misunderstanding, even of hatred, of Jews. I learned, with deep pain, of the responsibility of the Christian churches for what Jules Isaac was to call the Teaching of Contempt, a teaching which has contributed to the genocide of the Jewish people. From that day on I understood the urgency and importance of his mission. . . .

16. Bocquet, *Dans l'Amitié*, p. 4.

When spring came the two of us used to go for long walks in the countryside – he was a tireless walker. He would speak to me of his life: of the passionate commitments he had lived with his friend Péguy; of the Dreyfus Affair; of the Great War, and of his work as historian. And always he would come back to the subject that preoccupied him more than any other: Christian teaching about Judaism. Often, our walks would end with his invitation to me to read a text from one of the church fathers. Sometimes, after reading me aloud pages he had just edited, he would ask: "Is this too painful for your Christian sensibility? Am I being too harsh?" He was, indeed, harsh at times. But can you water down the truth?[17]

And so the cold, desolate winter passed, without news of those dear to Isaac. It was a subject never mentioned, the wound was too deep. Only in his "sacred mission" did he find courage and strength.

When spring came Paul Stern left for another Resistance network, believing it had become too dangerous for him to stay where he was. Soon after his departure the family was awakened one night by loud banging on the front door; lights appeared on the edge of the wood. They did not move, true to the rule they had made to give the appearance that the house was deserted. More banging, then the lights disappeared. They never knew what happened that night, but they decided to leave as soon as dawn came.

After a vain effort on Isaac's part to get to London – he was told by a member of the Resistance in charge of that operation, "there are already enough Jews in London!" – the decision was taken to ask Jacques' family for shelter; they lived in a small town already overflowing with refugees. Jacques' mother found a room for "uncle" in the town, a little more comfortable than his previous refuge. As to

17. *ibid.*

Germaine and Jacques, they moved in with two old ladies on the edge of town. Isaac immediately resumed his work in his new retreat, and Fr. Klein managed to continue to get him the necessary books. His new hosts soon became fond of him, they found that he resembled their nephew (so much for the imagination!, Germaine adds). He formed a friendship with a neighbor, a grocer who was a member of the Resistance, who was glad to have someone to listen to his ideas. "We often found him informally installed in the back of the store, giving M. Chastrette a course in economics. . . . At noon and in the evening we came together at my mother-in-law's" (*Dans l'Amitié*, p. 4).

Sunday afternoon they all gathered in his room and Isaac would read to them, for hours, from classical poets, "above all from his beloved Péguy. How can I ever forget his voice, celebrating 'this little Hope, who seemes to be nothing at all, this little daughter Hope, immortal. . . . '"

Gradually, more and more news about the camps began to reach the outside world. "We could barely imagine the horror. Only once did I see him give way to despair, but he quickly collected himself: 'I have my mission.' Finally, on June 6 [1944] the landing in Normandy, followed on August 25 by the liberation of Paris. Our own liberation came on August 28, our little town exploded in jubilation. Paul returned, alive and well" (p. 5).

But the rejoicing was premature. The Germans came back. Paul was captured, never to return. German soldiers entered the house, but finding only women and children left again. Isaac had fled to the woods behind the house barely in time. Hiding there, and seeing German soldiers enter, he was about to give himself up when they left.

After this last alarm the road to Paris was open and Isaac hastened to return there, hoping to find members of his family. He was reunited with his older son Daniel, who had been with DeGaulle's forces. It was several months before he learned that his younger son had survived Auschwitz and Dora; the rest of the family had perished.

Germaine writes: "I have tried, in these few pages, to recall our daily life with Jules Isaac during that short year when he was our 'uncle.'" The love which binds us to him since then remains faithful and deep. It continued to express itself throughout the years in his letters, in which he kept us abreast of the progress of his work, of his friendships, of the groups of *Amitié Judéo-chrétienne*. And we saw each other during the holidays, when we came home, year after year" [Germaine taught in Lebanon after the war]. "I always found a warm welcome in his house, the 'Perggola,' in Aix-en-Provence, the love of the 'old uncle,' as he liked to sign his letters. And the dialogue between us continued until his death.

"What he brought us through his love of truth, his nobility of soul, his invincible hope, his faithful friendship, remains engraved in the depths of our hearts and we thank God that, for too short a time, we had lived with one of the Just" (p. 7).

Germaine and Jacques Bocquet live quietly today in a secluded corner in the south of France. Their five children are grown, and fondly remember their "uncle." When, in July 1988, Germaine learned that she was to be honored by Yad Vashem as one of the Righteous among the Nations this was her response: "It is with deep emotion and gratitude that I read your letter, telling me of the great honor that will be conferred on me. . . . I am remembering all those who deserve this title far more than I do, because they laid down their lives. . . . I pray that peace may at long last flourish – in Israel and in the whole Middle East."[18]

In September 1994 Germaine was invited by Isaac's younger son, Jean Claude, to attend the opening, in the

---

18. Letter to Yad Vashem, July 7, 1988.

library of Aix-en-Provence, of a room named in honor of Jules Isaac. In this room are to be gathered all the books and documents concerning him, donated by his two sons.

Chapter Seven

A Prophetess of Penance and Renewal

MOST GERMANS WERE INITIALLY EITHER WILDLY ENTHU-
siastic about Adolf Hitler or adopted a wait-and-see attitude, but Gertrud Luckner saw through him from the very
beginning.

Thirty years of age when Hitler launched his national
political campaigns in 1930, Luckner, an unmarried social
work student, continued her studies during 1931 and then
visited her birth land, England in 1932. When she returned
to Germany, where she had lived since early childhood, it
was 1933. Hitler was already in power.

Stunned by the transformation that had swept over
the country in just one year, Luckner immediately began
to tell her Jewish friends and acquaintances to get out of
Germany.[1] No one else saw the murderous nature of Nazism as quickly as Luckner.

Certainly not the Vatican. While Luckner warned Jews
that they were in mortal danger, the Vatican awarded the
new Nazi regime a stamp of approval by hastily signing
an agreement or Concordat with Hitler.

---

1. Much of the material for this chapter comes from an interview of Gertrud
Luckner and Marie Schiffer by Dietrich and Ursula Goldschmidt, Barbara
Schieb, and Elizabeth von Thadden on 27 October, 1988, in Berlin. I am
indebted to Dietrich Goldschmidt for lending me the written transcript
of the interview.

After this, German bishops gave Catholics the green light to support Hitler, although just months earlier they had warned that Nazi racism would lead "to injustices which burden the Christian conscience." Luckner's own bishop, Conrad Gröber, was at first an active supporter of two Nazi organizations – the SA and the SS.

How was it possible for Gertrud Luckner to see through the Nazis so easily? How could she do so when the leaders of her church could not? Apparently, Luckner underwent an intense religious experience just at the time when Hitler achieved national prominence in 1930. It was at that time that she converted to Catholicism.

"Adopted" Catholicism may be more appropriate, for she did not abandon the pacifism, brotherliness, and humanitarianism of her Quaker upbringing. Very probably, Luckner did not feel that she had left the Quakers just by becoming a Catholic. She retained close contacts to her Quaker friends.

Perhaps, then, it was what Luckner brought to her Catholicism that allowed her to see Hitler and the Nazis for what they were long before church leaders did.

As Hitler consolidated his power in 1933, Luckner decided to return to the university to pursue a doctorate in social work. Did she hope in this way to avoid the Nazis? If so, it was to no avail. She enrolled in the University of Freiburg only to see it nazified by its apostate Catholic chancellor, Martin Heidegger.

The year that Luckner took her doctorate, 1938, was also the year when her prophecy regarding Jews became grim reality. In November German and Austrian Jews were beaten, imprisoned, and even killed (approximately 200). The events now known as *The Night of Broken Glass* were underway.

Jewish houses of worship were desecrated. Hundreds of synagogues were burned to the ground or burned beyond repair. The bishops now saw the error of the church's way, but they said nothing about the murder of the Jews and desecration of their religious houses.

Terrified, thousands of Jewish families fled Germany in 1938 and 1939. But thousands more were unable to flee for lack of money or a visa. Desperate and isolated, they had no choice but to remain in the hostile Nazi environment.

Determined not to abandon the Jews after the events of November, Luckner intensified her work. The dean of German Jews, Rabbi Leo Baeck, trusted Luckner and provided her with a list of contact people in Jewish communities throughout the country. They were so isolated, Luckner later recalled. "No one else visited them but me. They never forgot it."

Luckner soon became a known personality in Jewish circles around Germany. She often visited Berlin, where more Jews lived than anywhere else (190,000), and Munich, where the *Gauleiter* (regional Nazi party leader) was a notorious Jew-baiter. In the capital of Germany Luckner worked with Rabbi Baeck and with the group that formed around the priest, Bernhard Lichtenberg. In the capital of Bavaria, she worked with the Jesuit Alfred Delp, later executed by Hitler, who was actively helping Jews.

Luckner wanted to counter the Nazis by breaking through their extreme interior exile of the Jews. She went door to door visiting Jewish households, sometimes even spending the night. For this she was beaten by some Nazi youths, but it did not deter her, a diminutive woman who weighed less than 100 pounds.

When World War II began in 1939, Jews sensed that their situation was even more ominous. But the war made emigration almost impossible. Although Luckner had advised Jews to get out of Hitler's reach from the very beginning, she too now realized that the hour was more perilous.

This became painfully clear in 1941 when all Jews were forced to wear a yellow star of David on their outer clothing.

There were still many Jews in Germany who had converted to Catholicism in years gone by. They too had to wear the Star of David even when they went to church. Their embarrassment could have been averted had all the other "aryan" Catholics put on the yellow star as well. But this did not happen. Luckner did what she could by accompanying converted Jews to church to alleviate their feelings of exile, and she encouraged other Catholics to do likewise.

In acting this way Luckner was publicly going against what the Nazis intended to accomplish with the star decree. Church leaders themselves did not step forward to tell Catholics what they might or could do to make converts feel at one with them in Christ's church. Luckner acted alone.

After Hitler and Stalin had decided to divide Poland between them, Germany started World War II in the fall of 1939. The invasion of Poland led to immediate atrocities against Jews and their ghettoization.

Once the war began Jews nearly lost all hope of getting out of Germany. With the Nazis in control of much of Europe by the end of 1940, the situation was almost impossible. Tiny Switzerland became the only hope for many. Luckner's home base of Freiburg, just miles from the Swiss border, allowed her to exploit this situation. She secured as many Swiss visas as she could, and when they could not longer be obtained, Luckner assisted Jews in sneaking over the border.

Unfortunately, most of the Jews who had previously sought to escape Hitler by emigrating to a western European country were trapped again when Germany overran that part of the continent (except for Switzerland and the

Iberian peninsula). In 1941 and 1942 many of these hapless victims were also deported to eastern Europe and ghettoized.

The Nazis maintained that these Jews were simply being "resettled," but before long Luckner learned about their real fate from Margerete Sommer in Berlin. Starving and freezing in ghettos in Warsaw, Lodz and elsewhere in Poland, they were rapidly dying off. Luckner and others sent packages with food and clothing, but with little hope of relieving the misery of the uprooted Jews.

Luckner During the Holocaust's Early Phase

The murder of the Jews began in 1941 when Hitler, double crossing his ally Stalin, invaded Russia. Since the ghettos of western Poland were already vastly overpopulated, Hitler decided to kill Jews in eastern Poland and in Russia on the spot when the invading German army came upon them. Mobile Killing Squads (*Einsatzgruppen*) were formed, as we have seen, to accompany the army in conjunction with operation Barbarossa, the German invasion of Russia. Altogether these Mobile Killing Squads murdered between a million and a million and a half Jews during World War II.

Luckner found out about the gruesome killing process very soon, although the Nazis wanted it to be kept secret. The account of the Kovno massacres (see above, p. 33) is remarkably similar to the testimony of Otto Ohlendorf, one of the leaders of a killing squad, given at the Nuremberg trials after the war. Entire Jewish villages would be taken out into the countryside, forced to undress completely no matter what the weather conditions, and wait their turn to lie down in burial pits and be shot. Whole families – from grandparents to toddlers and infants in arms – met this fate together.

Many Germans, not wanting to know about these atrocities, disbelieved stories of mass murder. "What could I do?" was a common attitude. Luckner on the other hand wanted to know more. If Jews were being treated in this way, that was all the more reason to come to their assistance. Of course, no civilian would be allowed to go to the war zone where the murders took place, but word of the atrocities alarmed Luckner and increased her concern for western Jews who had been or were being ghettozied.

Luckner had reason to be alarmed. Sometime during 1941, most likely during the last half of the year, the Nazis made the decision to kill all European Jews, not just those in eastern Poland and in Russia. Naturally, only a few Nazis knew about this, but in 1942 Germans like Luckner who had been sending packages to ghettoized Jews found that their parcels went unacknowledged or were returned unopened. Thus, Luckner, who had stayed in touch with – among others – a *Herr* Meyer and his wife Gertrud, found that her packages and letters mailed to them at the Maidanek concentration camp in Poland were returned unopened.

Unbeknownst to Luckner and others the Nazis had built six death camps in Poland. In these facilities the Nazis murdered formerly ghettoized Jews. In four of them Jews were murdered immediately upon their arrival in railroad cattle cars. In two others, Maidanek and Auschwitz, they were either murdered immediately or put to intense slave labor until they were physically broken. Then they took their turn in the gas chamber.

If Luckner did not know that "transportation" to the east actually meant death, the mass murders of the killing squads and her unanswered mail told her to expect the worst. Luckner knew enough to know that she should rescue Jews before their "resettlement" in the east.[2]

The experience of the Rosenberg family illustrates Luckner's "not knowing-knowing" mental state. The father of the Rosenbergs had married a nonJew who bore two sons. According to Nazi law, the two boys were *Mischlingen* or half breeds (part aryan, part nonaryan). After the mother died, Rosenberg married again, this time choosing a Jewish wife who gave birth to a baby girl. When the Nazis began to "resettle" Jews in the east, the Rosenberg brothers, "half-Jews," became desperately concerned about their half-sister who was scheduled to be "transported."

The Rosenberg brothers asked Luckner what could be done to save their sister. Luckner, aware that the brothers had served in the army before being rejected as *Mischlingen*, referred them to a certain Günther, an adjutant of Adolf Eichmann, whom she knew to have a fondness for the military. As the brothers hurried to Berlin to make their plea, their sister had already been deported from Freiburg to Berlin where her "transportation" to the east was imminent. Luckner told the brothers to emphasize their military service, and to plea that their sister be sent to the camp at Theresienstadt instead of "to the east." The stratagem worked and the brothers' sister survived the Holocaust.

Clearly, Luckner did not yet know the full Holocaust story, but she knew enough to know that the Rosenberg girl would be better off in Theresienstadt than in a camp in Poland. She knew that Jews who were sent "to the east" were somehow in mortal danger. To Luckner this meant that she had to save as many as possible. This became her work during 1942. She hid Jews, helped them escape over the border into Switzerland, disabled trucks used for "transports," and got some of them redirected to Theresienstadt.

---

2. The words transportation and resettlement are put in parentheses to indicate their Nazi connotation of death.

Using her work for *Caritas* as an excuse, Luckner began traveling around Germany trying to get other Catholics to save Jews. While doing this Luckner made it her business to find out all she could about the Holocaust. On several occasions, Luckner decided to cross the border into Poland to find out for herself what was happening to the Jews who were being transported there. She succeeded in getting to Kattowitz, a city located in the immediate vicinity of Auschwitz.[3]

Luckner's last visit to Kattowitz took place early in 1943 at which point in time the new, modernized gas chamber-crematorium complexes were just being constructed at Birkenau (Auschwitz II).

Putting two and two together, Luckner might well have guessed why gas chambers were being constructed under the same roof as the crematoria. Shortly after this visit Luckner was arrested by the Gestapo. She breathed a sign of relief when she learned that she was not going to be sent to Auschwitz.

Luckner's efforts to engage Catholics nationally on behalf of Jews explains why she was constantly on the move during 1942 and 1943 visiting large German cities. Because of the war and the shortage of fuel, Germans were being encouraged either not to travel or to ride bicycles instead of taking a train. "Biking for Victory" signs were everywhere to be seen. After her arrest in 1943 an angry Gestapo agent scolded Luckner telling her that while other Germans were "biking for victory" she was "riding trains for Jews."

When the war turned decisively against Germany after the battles of Stalingrad in Russia during the winter of 1942-43 and El Alamein in Africa late in 1942, the Gestapo began to bear down on the population at home. No hint of

---

3. Jerzy Myszor, *Stosunki Kos'cio'l/ -Panstwo Okupacyjne W Diecezji Katowickiej, 1939- 1945* (unpublished ms: Katowice, 1992), 266.

resistance was tolerated. People who were ambitious or servile were encouraged to spy on their neighbors and report on them to the police. Luckner, who, like Sommer, was constantly under surveillance, was arrested in March, 1943, by the Gestapo while she was on a train bound for Berlin. She was carrying over one thousand dollars in German currency with her which she intended for distribution among Berlin's Jews.[4] But the actual reason for Luckner's arrest may have been her trip to Kattowitz near Auschwitz of which the Gestapo had taken note.[5]

Luckner's Imprisonment in the Ravensbrück Concentration Camp

With her arrest on 24 March, 1943, a two-year long, life-threatening ordeal began for Luckner. Initially, she was taken to Berlin, her interrogation beginning en route in the train. Afterwards Luckner was questioned daily for nine straight weeks; at one point she was grilled every night from six in the evening to eight in the morning for three weeks. The purpose of this was to discover what she and her bishop, Konrad Gröber of Freiburg, were doing on behalf of Jews.

At some point Luckner was taken from Berlin to Düsseldorf in western Germany for further detailed questioning. This gave rise to a bizarre, humorous event that Luckner recalled after the war. For the return trip to Berlin from Düsseldorf Luckner was guarded by a Gestapo agent who had packed his suitcase full of black market items. It was so full he could hardly lug it along the street on the way to the railroad station. Finally at the terminal, they learned that the train schedule had been changed making

---

4. Kurt R. Grossmann, "Gertrud Luckner," *Rheinischer Merkur*, no. 46 (Friday 13, Nov., 1970), p.4.

5. Myszor, p. 169.

a return trip to Berlin impossible on that day. Thereupon the exhausted Gestapo agent announced that they would just spend the night on the benches in the depot. Luckner however informed him that there was no way she would spend the night with him there, leaving him no alternative but to drag his loot back and forth to the station again.

Back in Berlin the decision was made to send Luckner to a concentration camp. Ernst Kaltenbrunner, chief of the Reich Security Main Office, personally signed her papers sending her permanently to prison, because "if she were released she'd work against the Reich again," on behalf of the Jews. Apprehensive, Luckner asked one of her guards to which concentration camp she would be sent, and was "somewhat relieved" to learn that it would be Ravensbrück not Auschwitz.

The Ravensbrück concentration camp for women proved frightful enough. The camp was supposed to accommodate about 7,000 but the actual number of prisoners exceeded capacity by several thousand. In Luckner's words, "the place was overflowing day and night." Living conditions and sanitation were atrocious, as in other concentration camps, causing a high death rate. Between 1939 and the end of the war around 90,000 women died there. Although Ravensbrück was not a death camp like Treblinka or Sobibor, there were "selections;" those who appeared weak or seriously sick were gassed and cremated. It was, as Luckner said, beyond imagination:

> People died constantly. And we ourselves had asked in the beginning about the gassing – was it a fact? . . . It [was] very hard for people to believe and grasp that it [was] really happening. Then, we saw the flames, right? . . . The flames came shooting out of the chimneys, as we stood there for the calling of the role – enormous flames that shot up to heaven day and night.

Luckner arrived at the camp in early November, 1943. Immediately, she had to undress and stand naked outdoors, along with the others in her group, for hours on end in the cold. Eventually, they were given filthy clothes to put on in place of their own. Luckner's were blood stained.

As at other concentration camps the routine at Ravensbrück included daily roll calls during which prisoners stood, sometimes for hours, exposed to the elements outside of their barracks. One night during one of the endless roll calls, Luckner struck up a conversation with a person in the line behind her. Recently, some Jewish prisoners from the Maidanek camp had been transferred to Ravensbrück, and Luckner explained to the person standing behind her that she had been corresponding with the Meyers until her letters and packages were returned unopened. Not able to turn to see to whom she was speaking, Luckner said,

> "I'd like to know what's going on there. And the voice behind me said in the darkness: 'Say the name once again.' I said, a Frau Gertrud Meyer. 'That's me!' the woman said."

Gertrud Meyer's husband had been gassed and cremated in the Maidanek camp. Thus did Luckner finally come to know what she had suspected for months: the extermination of Europe's Jews.

Life or death in Ravensbrück depended on helping others and on being helped by others. Luckner found herself in barrack number six, which was designated for the Communist prisoners. Her barrack mates, who had organized their own internal administration, accepted Luckner even though she was not one of them.

Often, Luckner later recalled, her Communist cell mates saved her life by putting her on work details that allowed her to escape death. Several times Luckner narrowly missed execution in the gas chambers. In July of 1944

Luckner was supposed to have been put on a "death transport" to Bergen-Belsen, where she would have been gassed, but her Marxist friends rescued her.

A sure ticket to the gas chamber was poor health. In Ravensbrück Luckner developed a large painful abscess on her neck, which constantly drained blood and matter. The camp doctor, losing patience with Luckner because the dressing kept coming off of the sore, shook her painfully and threatened to send her to the gas chambers. (He may actually have ordered her "transportation" as this episode took place in July when Luckner's cell mates kept her off the Berger-Belsen "transport.") Shortly thereafter, Luckner received a package from a Caritas acquaintance in Germany which contained, among foodstuffs like apples, some bandages.

Amazingly, such packages got through to Luckner now and then. Margarete Sommer, among others, remembered her and sent provisions which kept Luckner alive. At some point in 1944 Luckner developed severe intestinal influenza from which she never fully recovered. She was transferred to the barracks for the sick and dying where she lay, literally, between dead people amidst lice and filth. Luckner later said that she would not have survived this ordeal without the fruit that came along occasionally in the packages she was sent.

If others rescued Luckner, she did no less. One person, in particular, whom she was able to save was her pre-war friend *Frau* Gertrud Meyer. After their chance meeting in the dark during an *Appel* in the Ravensbrück compound, Luckner was separated from Frau Meyer who became very ill. All of Meyer's personal effects were taken from her and she was put into a special ward for the dying. Luckner smuggled provisions to her, including a night gown that she had gotten in the mail. The night gown protected *Frau*

Meyer from the cold, on account of which, she later stated, she was able to survive.

Looking back, we can see that Luckner's work was timely but short-lived. The systematic murder of the Jews was barely underway and had not as yet touched most German Jews when Luckner herself was arrested. Thus, she was already herself a victim of Nazi terror before the Holocaust developed in its full ghastly furor.

What had Luckner accomplished? In terms of saving life, very little. Only a few survivors of the Holocaust owed their good fortune to Luckner's endeavors.[6] This is not to be belittled of course. But there can be no talk of a systematic saving of life. The Caritas cells, which Luckner tried to engage "in almost every German city," to develop a rescue function, failed to do so.[7] Even in Berlin, where Margarete Sommer had a functioning rescue mission in operation, Caritas failed to become effectively involved.[8] Ultimately, most German Catholics turned their backs on the Jews in their hour of need.

But Luckner accomplished a great deal in terms of her postwar work. Above all, she saw and felt the spiritual depth of the Jewish people during their ordeal:

> The composure of the people, step for step, yes, its really the conviction of Jews as a people. . . .in the deepest sense. I just have to tell you – I will never forget it . . . with what composure they met the horror.

For the rest of her life Luckner's mind and heart were stamped by the memory of countless Jews going, spirits unbroken, to their death.

---

6. Deutschercaritasverband (henceforth, DCV), house archives, R 611 II; report on Luckner's 1950 visit to England.

7. Ibid.

8. Bistumsarchiv Berlin (henceforth, BAB), I/1-99, Sommer to Ludger Born, S.J.; n.p. 15 Sept, 47.

On the other hand, Luckner's Ravensbrück experience earned her the eternal respect of Jews. Because of her work for them she had to undergo the same fate as they – perilous existence in a concentration camp. In Ravensbrück death stalked her just as it did the Jews. Because of this the Jewish people returned the deep respect that she held for them. This bond became the foundation for Luckner's post-Holocaust work.

Providing for Survivors of the Holocaust

Hitler's end brought freedom for the few Jews who had survived the Holocaust and for Luckner. But not before one last Nazi atrocity – death marches. Luckner's began on the third of May, 1945, as the Russian troops advanced on Ravensbrück.

Just a few days later the war in Europe ended. Luckner pondered over what she should do with the rest of her life. At 45 years of age, in broken physical condition, without money, Luckner's thoughts turned to her birth land.

Postwar England was a paradise in comparison to Germany whose cities looked like open mausoleums and the people, like walking skeletons. Having just murdered between five and six million Jews, the country was spiritually dead.

Knowing all this why did Luckner choose Germany and trek hundreds of miles from somewhere in central Germany back to Freiburg? The answer is simple – the survivors of the Holocaust were huddled in displaced person camps in Germany where their own death marches had left them. They would eventually number 250,000 – all survivors of the Holocaust, now displaced persons. Having risked her life for Jews, Luckner would have found it impossible to abandon this remnant of humanity.

A letter Luckner received from Rabbi Leo Baeck – the very first letter from anyone after her release from Ravensbrück – encouraged her. The Berlin rabbi had himself survived the Holocaust and he never forgot that Luckner was on a mission to give him relief money when she was arrested. To Luckner the letter meant that her life had not been meaningless. And she knew that if she chose to continue in the same direction as before, she would be supported by her Jewish friends.

Back in Freiburg and once again in the employ of *Caritas*, two questions bore in on Luckner: how to help the survivors and how to make sure the Holocaust would never be repeated. The survivors needed immediate help; changing Germany's antisemitic ways, Luckner knew, would be an endless task.

It was returning German Jews, like Luckner's prewar friend Gertrud Meyer, whom Luckner wanted to help. She understood that what the German survivor needed even more than material support was moral support. And the moral support had to come from Germans, because fellow Germans had stood by or actually helped Hitler carry out the Holocaust.

But moral support proved difficult to muster. Germany after the war was awash in self-pity. The average German thought that for every Jewish Holocaust victim 10 Germans were killed by air raid bombs. Besides being preposterous, this attitude overlooked the fact that while Germans had been killed by the enemy, Jews had been murdered by their fellow countrymen.

Living on around 1,000 calories a day, Germans discovered what Jews had already learned in Hitler's concentration camps: most starving people can think only of food and only of themselves.

Once back home German Jewish survivors often felt unwelcome. There were exceptions. Michael Faulhaber, the

cardinal of Munich, wanted to charter a bus to bring his
city's Jews back from Theresienstadt. But another city,
Aschaffenburg, attempted to make its returning Jewish
citizens pay property taxes that were in arrears for the years
from 1938, when the synagogue had been destroyed, to the
end of the war![9]

Many German survivors returned to find their homes
had either been destroyed by bombs or been occupied by
Germans who now ate off their dishes, sat on their chairs
around their dining room tables, and slept in their beds.
Early in 1946 the Representative Body of Jewish Communities and Religious Associations (of Germany) wrote an
open letter to administrations of German states pointing
out that returning Jews still had not received back their
stolen property.[10]

Converted Jews, Hitler's victims no less than other
Jews, faced the additional problem of not being recognized
by international relief agencies as being eligible for support. Because of how welfare was traditionally organized
in Germany (by confession), Luckner cared for Catholic
Jews as an employee of *Caritas*. But her concern was for all
survivors.

Luckner knew that restitution was a matter of justice.
It could not wait until German antisemitism subsided. In
1948 Luckner got the Catholic bishops of Germany – a
powerful voice during the post-war occupation era – to call
for restitution.[11] At the same time she pressed Germany's
new state governments to speed up restitution.

Years after the war Luckner reminded her countrymen
that many survivors had not received a penny. In 1955

9. Frank Stern, *The Whitewashing of the Yellow Badge,* trans. William Templer
   (NY: Pergamon Press, 1992), 97.

10. Stern, 96-97.

11. Vera Bücker, *Die Schulddiskussion im deutschen Katholizismus nach 1945*
    (Bochum: Brockmeyer, 1989), ch. 3.

Luckner pointed out that 25,000 survivors, who had rights to restitution, had died without having been awarded any compensation. Of the remaining survivors 40% were over 60 and 33% were between 60 and 70.

Foot-dragging saved taxpayers' money! In fiscal year 1954-55 less than one percent of Germany's total budget was set aside for restitution.

With typical relentlessness Luckner campaigned tirelessly year after year to get Germany to do what was right and just for the survivors. Success finally came in 1956 when Germany's federal restitution system became operable.

Eradicating German Antisemitism

Luckner's immediate postwar goal was to care for Holocaust survivors, but she never lost sight of her long term ambition – curing her country of its antisemitism. To achieve it Luckner realized that she would have to function in and through her church.

The Cold War, beginning in the summer of 1947, worked against Luckner. It had the effect of distancing Germans further and further from their Nazi past as they were caught up in the defense of western Europe against communism. Overcoming antisemitism took on less and less importance for Germans at large and for the church. It was a discouraging time for Luckner; a time when she had to act on blind faith.

Luckner dug in her heels and prepared for a long campaign. She began gathering around her a circle of people who had authentic anti-Nazi credentials. Luckner's group soon realized that it was not enough to fight antisemitism: a new relationship between Jews and Christians had to be formed.

This necessitated breaking new ground theologically. But how was this to be accomplished at a time when Rome lacked interest in the question and looked with suspicion on interfaith relations?

Luckner decided to publish a journal, although she had no money and no church authorization to do so. For a woman, and a convert at that, to edit a journal that dealt with theological issues is rare today and unheard of in those times. Luckner possessed nothing with which to off-set these odds except her determination.

The first issue of the paper, which would ultimately reverse the attitude of the German church toward Jews and the Holocaust, appeared in August, 1948, under the title *Freiburger Rundbrief (The Freiburg Circular)*.[12]

The journal was to become Luckner's instrument for exposing antisemitism, preserving the memory of the Holocaust, creating dialogue, reviewing important literature and news events affecting Jews and Christians, and providing catechists and priests with useful copy for instruction.

During the first years of publication Luckner's crusade was a lonely one. Journal issues were irregular and sporadic because Luckner had to accumulate donations before going to press with each new number. The *Rundbrief's* writers were not compensated, a stressful problem because the postwar years were hungry times in Germany. The American occupational authorities liked the paper because it openly dealt with the problem of German antisemitism. But they provided only moral support, and in the eyes of

---

12. The full title ran "Freiburger Rundbrief zur Förderung der Freundschaft zwischen den Völkern des Alten und Neuen Testaments" (The Freiburger Rundbrief for Futhering Friendship between the Peoples of the Old and New Testaments). The title was altered slightly several times over the ensuing decades.

many Germans foreign approval made the *Rundbrief* suspect.

Hoping to pick up official church backing for her work, Luckner wrote to the Jesuit Robert Leiber, personal secretary and confidant to Pius XII. Explaining that her efforts met with indifference, passivity and resistance in Germany, Luckner asked if the Holy See would acknowledge the importance of the work of the *Freiburg Rundbrief*.[13]

Instead of support, the Vatican responded by investigating Luckner. In 1948 the Holy Office issued a *monitum*, an official warning, against Luckner's pro-Jewish work. Fighting antisemitism, Rome said, was leading to religious indifferentism (one religion is as good as the next).

Undaunted, Luckner pushed ahead exposing antisemitism and fighting against it. Jewish cemeteries were being defaced in practically all major cities. In one state alone there were more than 200 incidents in 1950. After 12 years of Nazi indoctrination, many Germans had become accustomed to racist jargon ("non-aryan," "mixed breed"), and continued to use it. School children unwittingly mouthed Nazi racist slurs.

Luckner and her Freiburger circle were especially concerned about Catholic antisemitism embedded in popular devotion. In one south German city an annual procession still took place to recall an alleged defilement of the sacred host by Jews during the Middle Ages! The famous Passion play at Oberammergau was another case in point. Luckner discovered that all of the actors in the play with one exception were former members of the Nazi party.

While fighting antisemitism, Luckner's circle of associates pioneered Christian-Jewish dialogue. Not herself theologically schooled, Luckner depended on the talents

---

13. Institut für Zeitgeschichte ED 163/48; Luckner to Leiber; Freiburg, 31 March, 1949.

of others in this regard. Still, it was her reputation and that alone which made Jews willing to dialogue at all after the Holocaust, and which attracted leading Jewish savants like Martin Buber.

Dialogue could only begin after Christians put aside certain inherited fabrications and misunderstandings. A survivor of the Holocaust, Jules Isaac, whom we have already met in connection with the French woman Germaine Bocquet, challenged Christians to drop their prejudices in his book *Jesus and Israel*. In 1950 Luckner joined with other Catholics and Protestants to formalize Isaac's challenge into 10 assertions which became known as the Seelisberg Theses. By adopting this statement Luckner's group created an atmosphere for dialogue that was acceptable to both Jews and Christians.

Luckner's circle was able to sustain dialogue with close-minded Catholics and with Jews through their openness. Their frankness and willingness to discuss religious differences of opinion were unusual qualities for the time.

These same qualities allowed Luckner herself to change. Her original motivation behind the help she gave Jews was to convert them. She may be faulted for not being forthright about this fact, although it was entirely typical of the times. Through the process of dialogue, however, both Luckner and the Freiburg group underwent a genuine transformation.

By the mid-1950s they had begun to see that the covenant between God and the Chosen People was still valid. Once this stage had been reached, Luckner's circle thought more and more in terms of a coexistence of the "Two People of God."

Luckner was well aware that she and her associates were breaking new ground with these ideas. In 1950 she received a letter from an irate Catholic subscriber to the *Rundbrief* which she answered painstakingly, because she

realized that most Germans held the view of her correspon-
dent, namely, that the covenant between God and his People had been suspended by their rejection of the Messiah.
Luckner responded that this is a mistaken idea since God
never withdrew his covenant.

This idea was quite controversial in 1950 but it had to
be defended.[14] It was not enough for Catholics simply to
put their negative attitudes toward Jews behind them.
There had to develop in addition the concept of the intrinsic
value of Judaism as a faith and its positive contribution to
Christianity. Without this vital step, according to another
pioneer in ecumenism, Cardinal John Willebrands, it would
not have been possible to create the basis for future Catholic-Jewish understanding.

Nostra Aetate: Catholic-Jewish Reconciliation

To Luckner and her friends progress in their work seemed
glacially slow. Few people subscribed to a journal like
theirs that promoted such a isolated and embarrassing
cause as Catholic-Jewish relations. While some of her associates became discouraged, Luckner plodded on avoiding politics and personality conflicts.

Luckner always displayed a pragmatism and hard-
headedness in her work. Difficult as it was for a woman to
influence ecclesiastical affairs, Luckner continued to work
through church channels. Her objective was to sensitize the
younger generation of German bishops who were gradually replacing the prelates of the Nazi era as they died. She
wished above all to sensitize them to the Holocaust itself
during an era when most of Germany studiously avoided
this topic.

---

14. Eva Fleischner, *Judaism in German Christian Theology Since 1945*
(Metuchen: Scarecrow press, 1975), 24-69.

Luckner's faith and persistence gradually overcame passivity and won over the younger bishops. This suddenly became apparent at the end of the decade of the 1950s when Germans, reversing themselves 180 degrees, became intensely interested in the Holocaust. After years of a deadening silence, German radio, television, and the print media were suddenly all over the subject of the Holocaust.

More than anything else it was the Eichmann trial in Jerusalem that electrified Germany. In 1960, just when public opinion had become aroused over the Holocaust, Adolf Eichmann was put on trial in Israel charged with masterminding the murder of millions of Jews. Eichmann's trial provided Germans for the first time since the Nuremberg trials with an overview of the totality of human slaughter that had come to be known as the Holocaust.

With the nation's focus now riveted on the Holocaust, Germans heard Eichmann's chief prosecutor, Gideon Hausner, suggest that the Vatican had known about the Holocaust, but that Pope Pius did not speak out about it because of sensitivity to the predicament in which it would have placed German Catholics. With that, the conduct of the church itself during the Nazi era and in connection with the Holocaust became a matter of public debate in Germany.

Gertrud Luckner had always known that Catholics and the church had not reacted vigorously, to say the least, during and after the Holocaust. But she also knew that it would be fatal for her cause to point accusatory fingers. Now, however, with the discussion about the church launched from other quarters, Luckner gave it great play in her journal. Almost every German family, Luckner noted, was hotly questioning and discussing their country's past. The stage was set once again for the church's response.

It marked a turning point. The church exchanged its garments of triumphalism for those of penance. At the outset of the trial bishop – later Cardinal – Julius Döpfner published an open letter in which he told in graphic detail about the murder of a specific group of Romanian children who were exterminated after a cruel period of waiting. It shames us, Döpfner concluded, that this took place in the Christian west. Another bishop, Franz Hengsbach of Essen said, we "know, clearly or not so clearly, that all of us have a share in the sin [of all atrocities]."

Hengsbach and Döpfner were two of the bishops who had responded positively over the years to Luckner's crusade for Catholic-Jewish relations. In May, 1960, Bishop Hengsbach had written to Luckner encouraging her to keep up her important work.

In 1961 Luckner's influence was felt nationally in Germany. The bishops directed that on Sunday, June 11, a prayer for the persecuted Jews, which Luckner's group had provided, should be offered in all of the nation's Catholic churches. It read, in part,

> we confess before You that millions of persons in our midst were murdered because they belonged to the race from which the Messiah took on flesh . . . We beseech You: teach all those among us, who are guilty through deed, omission, or silence, understanding and conversion.[15]

Just as the Eichmann trial was stirring deep waters in Germany, winds of change blew through the Vatican. In 1959 Pope Pius' was succeeded by John XXIII, who, wanting to reinvigorate faith, called a plenary council. Seeing this, Jules Isaac decided to try to bring the matter of Christian antisemitism to Pope John's attention just as he had

---

15. Rolf Rendtorff and Hans Hermann Henrix, eds, *Die Kirchen und das Judentum* (Paderborn: Bonifatius press, 1988), p. 242.

ten years earlier – for naught – when Pius XII ruled the church.

In June of 1960 Isaac talked with Pope John who spontaneously accepted the French survivor's idea for the council to review Catholic-Jewish relations, and sent Isaac himself to Cardinal Bea, the German Jesuit in charge of drafting the council's statement on non-Christian religions. Bea was a pioneer in ecumenism in his own right.

The great majority of the German bishops who took part in the Second Vatican Council had been consecrated in the post-Nazi era and had been much more receptive to Luckner's work than their predecessors of Hitler's time. When the moment came during the council to debate Catholic-Jewish relations, these bishops were driven by their memory of the Holocaust to redress the church's ancient antisemitism.

The Council struggled for many years with its statement on the Jews. Draft after draft was debated. There were a number of problems but the most difficult single issue was the very question that Luckner and her circle had fought against for so many years – the idea that Jews were a cursed race for rejecting their Messiah.

When a draft was finally ready for ratification in 1964 as the council was nearly over, it was again jeopardized on purely tactical grounds concerning Christians living in Moslem countries. At this critical juncture a German bishop, Joseph Stangl, gave an electrifying address. Making direct reference to the recent sensational play, *The Deputy*, by the German playwright Rudolph Hochhuth, Stangl told the Council fathers that a storm of debate had arisen in Germany concerning the conduct of the pope and the German church during the Holocaust.

Now, Stangl affirmed, the moment of truth was upon the Council. Would it choose the way of candor and justice or the way of tactics and diplomacy? Using the same word that Hochhuth had chosen for the title of his play, Stangl declared, "If we speak in the name of God, in the name of Jesus Christ, as the *deputies* of the Lord, then our message must be clear 'Yes, yes! (or) No, no' – the truth, not tactics."[16]

Stangl's moving address provided the impetus for adopting the statement on the Jews, *Nostra Aetate*, in the last hours of the Council. Precisely because of the Holocaust, German bishops welcomed the statement saying "that we are aware of the awful injustices that were perpetrated against the Jews in the name of our people."[17]

The Second Vatican Council marked at one and the same time a vindication and culmination of Gertrud Luckner's pioneer work. Having suffered through the years of Nazi persecution of the Jews, Luckner lived to see her church cleanse itself of antisemitism and embrace its Judaic heritage.

16. Rendtorff, 463-64.
17. Rendtorff, 243.

Chapter Eight

The Women Who Cared: Did They Make a Difference?

THE CHRISTIAN CHURCHES OF EUROPE WERE UNABLE TO prevent the Holocaust. Raul Hilberg's humbling judgment that the churches had become nothing more than the time keepers of Europe, marking sacramentally the milestones of life, is numbing. But the verdict cannot be challenged. It applies especially to the Catholic church, since the Holocaust took place in predominantly Catholic eastern Europe.[1]

Thus it is that from an historical point of view the women we have written about in these chapters constitute no more than footnotes to the Holocaust's terrible record of human destruction. What we have written does not alter this record. We have remembered these seven Christian rescuers because they are our hope for our faith in God and human kind.

Fifty Years of Silence Broken

Why has it taken so long – a half century in fact – for the stories of these seven women to be written? Both Jewish and non-Jewish historians have asked why the Christian community has not stepped forward to claim its heroes

---

1. Raul Hilberg, *Perpetrators, Victims, Bystanders*. New York: HarperCollins, 1992, pp. 260-61.

and heroines.[2] Just answering this question places us in an awkward, uncomfortable situation.

First of all, Hilberg's judgment provides an immediate response: it is painful to draw attention to ourselves because the Holocaust took place in the Christian West where the disproportion between the relatively few rescuers and the many collaborators is plain for all to see.

Equally confounding for the Christian community is the fact that religious teaching inspired people to help Jews no more frequently than other motives such as anger at the Germans or compassion for children.[3] We may only hope that beneath these emotions lay a foundation of Christian morality.

In addition, there is an historical reason for the silence. The postwar triumphalism of the Catholic church, though totally uncalled for, drew attention away from Catholic rescuers, like Margarete Sommer, whose behavior was even downplayed. The dean of German bishops, Cardinal Josef Frings, went so far as to assert that those who resisted Nazism had foolishly put themselves at the mercy of Nazi barbarism.[4]

Even if the church had been repentant after the war, it would have been difficult for it to praise those members who had heroically saved Jews. How could the German church claim Luckner and Sommer as models of Christian behavior after not having held up the Scholls, the Delps, the Lichtenbergs and the Jägerstätters for emulation during the Holocaust?

---

2. Lawrence Baron, "The Historical Context of Rescue," 13-48 of Samuel P. and Pearl M. Oliner, *The Altruistic Personality. Rescuers of Jews in Nazi Europe*. New York: Free Press, 1988; and David P. Gushee, *The Righteous Gentiles of the Holocaust*. Minneapolis: Fortress Press, 1994. See the preface.

3. Gushee, pp. 75 and 100.

4. Marquette University archives, Riedl papers; box 2: the Catholic Church and Nazism; see the interview with OMGUS officer, Richard G. Akselrad.

The situation was similar, or worse, in postwar Poland. Those who have written about Mother Matylda Getter note that after the war no one spoke about her work. In fact, four decades passed before Getter began to be praised publicly. Why? Those Catholics who helped Jews during the Holocaust found that their neighbors held their rescue efforts against them after the war. One researcher has discovered that Poles risked physical abuse or even death if fellow Christians found out about their protection of Jews during the Holocaust.[5]

At first it appeared that in France there would be more openness. Disgusted with the church hierarchy because of its comfortable association with the Vichy government, Charles DeGaulle attempted to have over twenty bishops dismissed.[6] He also appointed the man who had acted as the Christian conscience of the free world during the Holocaust, Jacques Maritain, as ambassador to the Vatican. But Maritain's voice fell upon deaf ears in Rome, and in France it soon proved more comfortable to wear the hat of a victor than of the Nazi collaborator. Thus, as in Germany, French Catholic rescuers like Germaine Ribière and Germaine Bocquet became an embarrassment, rather than the pride of the nation.

Finally, guilt is also a factor contributing to the long silence. Guilt troubled many rescuers and kept some of them from speaking out openly after the Holocaust. Ribière was able to deal with this by referring to the shortcomings of the Catholic church and, remarkably, by associating herself as a member of the church with this guilt. But Sommer could not do so. Like Ribière and other rescuers, Sommer was bothered by the fact that she had not been

---

5. Eva Fogelman, *Conscience and Courage. Rescuers of Jews during the Holocaust*. New York: Anchor Books, 1994, 273ff.

6. Erich Klausener, *Von Pius XII zu Johannes XIII*, Berlin: Morus Verlag, 1958, 79.

able to do more in the face of the Holocaust.[7] Unlike Ribière, Sommer internalized her guilt. This led her to review critically and scrupulously her own deeds during the Holocaust era until the end of her life more than 20 years later.

Not without reason then has the Christian community kept silent about its heroines. David Gushee's words strike close to the heart: "Royal priesthood? Holy nation? Community of saints? Transformed people of God? First fruits of God's new creation? How broad and deep is the gulf between who we are in Christ and who we were during the Holocaust."[8] These pungent words say it all.

Are Holocaust Rescuers Christian Models?

Having said all this, what is the significance of these seven women? Can or should Christians hold them as models of behavior? Yes, because their motivation for their action was intensely religious.

Nevertheless, the "yes" must not stand without some qualification. Non-Christian rescuers or dissenters, like Communists, endured the same fate as our seven Catholic rescuers. The Gestapo dogged Margarete Sommer in Berlin and was only two steps behind the Bocquets in southern France, but this was a danger to which all rescuers of Jews exposed themselves. In Limoges, France, Ribière tried to intervene personally to stop transports of Jews, as did Luckner in Freiburg, Germany; this kind of risk-taking was not exceptional for the righteous in general. Fear gripped the elderly mother superior Getter, but in Poland all rescuers put their lives and the lives of their families on the line. Margit Slachta was beaten in Hungary by collaborators and her life was in mortal danger, but many resisters or rescuers

---

7. Fogelman, 79.
8. Gushee, 175.

experienced the same treatment and not a few actually met
their deaths.

We see that in most respects our seven Christian righteous women cannot be distinguished from all of the other
heroes and heroines honored by Yad Vashem. Gertrud
Luckner is somewhat of an exception. Only a relatively few
non-Jews experienced what Jewish victims faced in concentration camps. In Ravensbrück Luckner endured lice,
filth, naked degradation, life threatening selections, and
existence in the shadow and stench of the crematoria.

But Luckner is the exception which proves the rule.
The rescuers in the lion's den were a very heterogeneous
group of people who, taken collectively, had all suffered
under Nazi rule. Thus, if we are to take the Ribière's and
the Sommer's as our Christian models, we do so with a
sense of honesty and humility. Not only were Christian
rescuers few in number but their deeds were matched by
rescuers whose motivations were not specifically Christian
or were not so at all.

The Holocaust and Nostra Aetate

In one significant respect our Catholic women stand apart
from other rescuers. Each of them worked within the institutional church. In Poland Getter integrated her help for
Jews into her life work for children. Gineste in France was
already in the service of her diocese when she volunteered
for the work that became the most exhilarating of her life.
Four of the other women not only worked within the church
but sought to provoke a stronger institutional response to
the Holocaust. In the final analysis they succeeded. Let us
consider this relationship in some detail.

Ribière in France, Luckner and Sommer in Germany,
Slachta in Hungary, all pressed church authorities to engage the church on behalf of the Jews. Particularly note-

worthy is the fact that they did this early on, that is, well before genocide itself occurred. Since they had seen Nazi antisemitic policy unfold during the 1930s, Luckner and Sommer were among the first to take action to help Jews. Slachta began working in 1940 on behalf of Jews who faced dispossession and deportation from Hungary. Ribière wrote in a May, 1941, entry in her journal that "Those who should keep watch are the ones who put others to sleep."

What was it that these women expected of their church leaders? They clearly wanted the official church to speak out forcefully and unequivocally. They wanted an end to discretion, to what Ribière called "this ridiculous prudence." Though just a young university student, Ribière did not shrink from contacting important bishops like Gerlier and Saliège. Eventually, she had the satisfaction of hearing some French bishops speak out against the Holocaust.

In spite of their urgent prodding, Slachta and Sommer could not get the bishops of Hungary and Germany to denounce Nazi crimes. Their only hope was that the pope himself would break his silence on behalf of the Jews. But Slachta's Roman visit bore no fruit. It appears that Pius XII thought to use the occasion of Slachta's audience merely to silence her conscience, rather than to break his own silence.

It is often asked if it would have made any difference had the pope spoken out. The answer, it seems to us, is a clear "yes." At the time a forceful papal denunciation of the murder of the Jews would have changed what Nechama Tec has called the *moral ambiguity* of Catholics regarding the Jewish predicament. (See Tec's impressive study, *When Light Pierced the Darkness* published by Oxford University press.) Catholics, Tec has reasoned, were morally ambiguous because on the one hand their church taught contempt for Jews as Christ killers but, on the other hand, that murder was sinful. Moral ambiguity led Catholics to respond to the Holocaust in extreme ways – some as rescuers but many others as Nazi collaborators. Had Pius XII ended this ambiguity by denouncing the murder of the Jews, it is reasonable to conclude that there would have been more rescuers and fewer collaborators. More Jews would have survived the Holocaust.

Nevertheless, two of the women rescuers we have discussed, Bocquet and Luckner, were instrumental in ending the church's antisemitic teachings for all time. It was Germaine Bocquet who rescued Jules Isaac. Bocquet had no idea that while she sheltered Isaac he would write *Jesus and Israel,* the book that was subsequently to revolutionize Catholic-Jewish relations. It was happenstance, reminiscent of Miep Gies harboring of Anne Frank in Holland. Still, the fact that a Catholic woman would serendipitously rescue Isaac does not lessen the historical importance of Bocquet's action.

Except for Jules Isaac's persistence, Jewish-Catholic relations might never have come under review by the Second Vatican Council in the early 1960s. In vain Isaac attempted a few years after the Holocaust to persuade Pius XII to adopt the principles of *Jesus and Israel* and put an end to Christian antisemitism. Ten years later Isaac visited Rome a second time and found that the new pope, John XXIII, responded with spontaneous enthusiasm to his suggestions. The conciliar document that resulted from Isaac's proposal, *Nostra Aetate,* finally ended the church's negative teaching about Jews.

By way of contrast to Bocquet, Gertrud Luckner's intervention in Catholic-Jewish relations was planned and pursued step by step. It fell to Luckner to propagate the ideas that Isaac had recorded in *Jesus and Israel* among the postwar generation of German bishops. She did this, as we have seen, relentlessly during the 1950s. It is not an exaggeration to say that Luckner prepared the bishops for the role they were to play regarding the Jews during the Second Vatican Council.

It turned out to be a crucial role. Because of *Nostra Aetate*'s reversal of negative teaching about Jews reaching back to the time of the church Fathers, the bishops at the council hotly debated one draft after another of the document. In the end it would not have been adopted had not the German bishops, who had been tutored by Luckner, unanimously supported it.

Since Catholic women lack any official voice in their church, it is remarkable that Bocquet and Luckner were able to play central roles in the church's historic break with antisemitism. Even more remarkable is the fact that there can still be hope for lasting Jewish-Christian reconciliation after the Holocaust.